An Anthropological Study
of Hospitality

Amitai Touval

An Anthropological Study of Hospitality

The Innkeeper and the Guest

Amitai Touval
Baruch College
CUNY
New York, USA

ISBN 978-3-319-42048-6   ISBN 978-3-319-42049-3 (eBook)
DOI 10.1007/978-3-319-42049-3

Library of Congress Control Number: 2016956246

Cover illustration: Pattern adapted from an Indian cotton print produced in the 19th century

Printed on acid-free paper

This Palgrave Macmillan imprint is published by Springer Nature
The registered company is Springer International Publishing AG
The registered company address is: Gewerbestrasse 11, 6330 Cham, Switzerland

ACKNOWLEDGMENTS

I would like to thank those who made it possible to conduct research in Leipzig: the German Academic Exchange, the Watson Institute, and Brown University's Graduate School. I would also like to thank Prof. Steven Cerf of Bowdoin College and my teachers of German at the Goethe Institute (Boston), Brown University and the Herder Institute, (Leipzig). This manuscript greatly benefited from the editorial guidance of Miles Becker. His advice and comments made an enormous difference. I am grateful to Franco Burgio for his feedback, Josué Ramirez, Tatiana Aloi Emmanouil, and Lily Shen for their incisive comments, and Brinton Ahlin, Jill Twark and Benjamin Folkman for their lists of references. I would like to thank Prof. Chung-fu Chang for the opportunity to present a version of the first part of this book at a seminar at the Department of Ethnology, National Chengchi University, Taipei. I am grateful for his comments as well as the comments of Profs. Ya-ning Kao, Da-wei Kuan, and Fen-fang Tsai. Lastly, I would like to thank my Airbnb hostess and the innkeeper and his family for teaching me some valuable lessons; the librarians at the New York Public Library, where I conducted much of the secondary research; and my friends and family for encouraging me to complete this manuscript. I am also grateful for the assistance of Mireille Yanow, Milana Vernikova, Nicholas Byrne, Kyra Saniewski and Alexis Nelson of Palgrave Macmillan, the contribution of Preeju Prasad, Sruthi Surendran and Ramesh Ganesan to the editorial process, and for the comments of the anonymous reviewer. However, I bear sole responsibility for any errors or shortcomings in this manuscript.

CONTENTS

CHAPTER 1

The Innkeeper

Abstract In 1996, I stayed at a small apartment-based inn in Leipzig, eastern Germany. The innkeeper, Herr Klaus, was an aging widower. In his practice of hospitality, he adhered to three values: economizing, advising his guests, and standing on the side of local authorities.

I consider Herr Klaus's inn within the history of hospitality in East Germany, and reflect on his diminished circumstances in the aftermath of German unification.

Depending on the situation, Herr Klaus expressed these values to reward or punish his guest.

Drawing on the anthropological record, I speculate that traditions of hospitality that allow hosts to express hostility are more resilient than ones that require hosts to be always generous and protective of their guests.

Keywords Hospitality · Innkeeper · East Germany · Hostility · Advising · Economizing

ARRIVING AT THE INN

I unloaded my suitcases from the airport bus outside Leipzig's monumental train station. Some hangers-on by the telephone booths were pestering pedestrians between cigarette puffs. Leaning over my suitcases, I held a grimy telephone handset to my ear. The streetcars were screeching horribly, but I could hear Herr Klaus, the innkeeper, loud and clear. "No need for a taxi!" he said, laughing.

© The Author(s) 2017
A. Touval, *An Anthropological Study of Hospitality,*
DOI 10.1007/978-3-319-42049-3_1

Herr Klaus's advice would spare me the expense of a cab, though I disliked his jocular laugh, its ring of derision. But I was in a good mood. The sun was out, and the October air was cool and fresh. It was wonderful to be back in Leipzig.

I reached a corner building, five stories high and perhaps a century old, at the southern end of a neighborhood full of charming old buildings just like it. The classical exterior, which clearly had not been painted in years, was accentuated by triangles and arches sculpted in relief over tall windows, suggesting wide and well-lit rooms with high ceilings. I slowly pushed open the elegantly carved wooden door, stepped inside, and began searching for mailboxes in the hope of finding Herr Klaus's name. When I looked up at the wall, scanning the peeling paint for clues, I found a big board that announced the name of each of the residents in fancy Gothic script. My innkeeper was on the third floor.

Herr Klaus was about 65, a large man wearing slippers and a gray sleeveless sweater. We shook hands and he helped me navigate my suitcases into a long, narrow room. Looking at the grand exterior of this building from the outside, I had not imagined that some of its bedrooms were no wider than a single window. Along the left wall of the room were two beds lined up one after the other, and on the right wall was a small desk with a chair next to an armoire. I stepped back to let him open the armoire, and he took out a hanger for my coat. I walked back into the corridor to let him out of the room. "Let me show you one more thing," he said, before walking to a door across the hall from the bedroom. He opened the door and turned on a light to illuminate a small room containing a toilet and a miniature sink. It was a stark, cold space with a high ceiling. Herr Klaus reached for a cord hanging from the water tank that was suspended high above the toilet, then pulled it down, releasing a stream of water. "You only need to tug once, and gently." He turned to me. "Not like that," he said, jerking his hand down abruptly.

I confidently nodded in agreement. After all, Frau Henneke, my landlady of the summer before last, had done the same thing. After showing me to my room, she had demonstrated precisely how to flush the toilet. In fact, their two apartments had a similar layout: an entrance hall with three doors on the right and three on the left. Herr Klaus now led me to a door opposite the entrance, which was the bathroom.

"When do you take a bath?"

"In the evening."

"Very well, then. For your information, 45 minutes before you take a bath, turn this on." He pressed a switch, which turned red.

FIELDWORK AND THE INTERACTION OF HOSTS AND GUESTS

The basis of the first part of this book is nine days that I spent with Herr Klaus, an innkeeper in Leipzig, at the end of October 1996. I had found a listing for Herr Klaus's inn in a popular English-language guidebook at a Borders bookstore in White Flint Mall (Kensington, Maryland) some weeks earlier. I was preparing to start my anthropological fieldwork in Leipzig at the time, and I was looking for a temporary place to stay until longer-term accommodations could be found. I arrived at the inn on October 24, 1996, and I left there on November 2, 1996, to move into an apartment that I had rented in a neighborhood of prefabricated buildings ten minutes west of downtown. I had met other innkeepers during my stay in Germany, and I had heard stories about German hospitality from friends and family members, but hospitality was not the focus of my work at the time. The purpose of my visit to the country was to conduct research on the impact of German reunification on people's lives. I would be attending public events organized by various associations and by the city government, and I would be interviewing friends and acquaintances, members of various associations, representatives of the East German intelligentsia, and both current and socialist-era politicians about their lives before, during and after the peaceful revolution of 1989 (Touval 2005, 2011, 2013). While I did not consider this spell of nine days at Herr Klaus's inn in October 1996 to be part of my fieldwork, I nonetheless took careful notes on my experiences there, notes which I later expanded into the following narrative—although it is important to state at the outset that the conversations I recount here are not direct quotations, but rather reconstructions based on these notes and my memories. I revisited the neighborhood where the inn was located on subsequent visits to Leipzig in 2000, 2007, and 2015. It is only in the past few years, however, that I contemplated mining this experience for its broader significance (Touval 2014).

I define hospitality as a series of transactions between individuals playing the roles of host and guest. Beliefs and values complicate this interaction and inform the judgments of everyone involved in it. Hosts and guests are never *only* hosts and guests to each other; their many other roles and identity markers are always there in the background, coloring their intentions and the meanings attributed to them and to their actions. Indeed, the very designations of "host" and "guest" assume that the individuals who take on these roles engage each other's understanding of how they are related to the social space in which hospitality is rendered. This understanding, in turn, helps individuals navigate the infinite variety of questions that may emerge in such social spaces: is this my home, or yours?[1] When I picnic or camp on this plot of land, am I your guest, a passerby, or an intruder? If I am attending your wedding and am surrounded by my own family and friends, can I take this opportunity to celebrate, simultaneously, my birthday? Hospitality overlaps with, often ritually confirms, but sometimes also challenges the complex assumptions embedded in the legal and or political institutions that map people's standing in relation to each other and the social space around them.

One of my main findings is that Herr Klaus's interaction with his guests was informed by three primary values: that guests should be provided with the comforts and provisions that they deserve, but no more; that an innkeeper should give advice to his guests; and that an innkeeper should stand on the side of local authorities. The actions through which Herr Klaus expressed these sometimes overlapping values could sometimes be rewarding and pleasing to guests, but at other times could seem hostile.[2] As we shall see, Herr Klaus's economizing sensibility and his penchant for giving advice actually brought the two of us together before finally pushing us apart.

A WALK IN DOWNTOWN: VIOLENCE AND RHETORIC

After Herr Klaus had showed me around the apartment, I decided to go out for a walk. In the downtown pedestrian zone of Grimmaische Street, I saw a group of people distributing pamphlets. They wore woolly sweaters and were advocating vegetarianism. Next to their table stood a small mechanical crane, which I at first assumed was construction-site clutter, so much of which littered the city that a walk downtown would turn into an obstacle course of unpaved sidewalks and detours around dug-up water mains and webs of scaffolding. But this small crane seemed to be drawing bystanders' attention. Shielding my eyes against the sun, I looked up at the object dangling from its arm. And I could not believe what I saw: a dead brown cow, bound by the feet, was suspended upside down above the sidewalk. I looked again at the booklet that I had collected from the pamphleteers' information table, and I realized that the photo on the cover featured the same gruesome scene: the corpse of cow hanging from a crane.

I hurried off to the post office across Augustus Square, upset by the gratuitous violence of the vegetarians. The dead cow was both a symbol and an actual instance of a barbaric act against an animal. Why did they have to be so literal? Making something so literal out of a metaphor violated the spectators' trust. It seemed a cheap device for attracting attention, a rhetorical tactic that ultimately depended on the very violence they were condemning. The violence blurred the boundary between the actual dead cow, dangling unceremoniously a few feet above the pavement, and the meaning that this spectacle was intended to communicate: that the cow could be a symbol of all animals that are in need of protection from violence.

This rhetorically sophisticated but cruel channeling of violence immediately reminded me of certain plays that I had seen in the highly respected Neue Szene (New Scene) Theater two summers before. The actors struck each other, and bodily injuries were depicted in a particularly gruesome way. The violence on stage seemed so real that it challenged the boundary between literal and metaphorical meaning.

HOSPITALITY IN GERMANY AND OTHER CULTURES

In German hospitality, the two most common words for host are *Gastgeber* and, in the context of inns and restaurants, *Wirt* (Clark and Thyen 2005: 287; Seebold 2002: 993). The verb *bewirten* means to give food and drink to a guest (Duden 2010: 218). *Wirt* is closely related to the word *Wirtschaft*, which translates to the noun "economy" but can also refer to a simple or ordinary restaurant (Duden 2010: 1099). While Herr Klaus was both *Gastgeber* and *Wirt*, he also used the word *Pension* to describe his inn, so I think a third, less common term, *Pensionsinhaber* ("pension owner"), is the label that fits him best.

The most general German word for hospitality is *Gastfreundschaft* (Clark and Thyen 2005: 287). More technically, there is a distinction in the literature between *Gastfreundschaft*, meaning hospitality as friendly and inclusive sociability, and *Gastlichkeit*, meaning hospitality as service-like interaction (Pechlaner and Raich 2007: 14, 17). While some dictionaries define *Gastlichkeit* as synonymous with *Gastfreundlichkeit* (Wahrig-Burfeind 2000: 519), the distinction between the terms is observed in the German professional literature on hospitality management. Harald Pechlaner and Frieda Raich (2007), for example, urge a better integration of *Gastlichkeit* and *Gastfreundschaft* as a means of improving the quality of inns, hotels and other tourist destinations in Germany. Viewing the issue historically, some authors define *Gastfreundschaft* as emblematic of the hospitality, suffused with Christian and courtly ideals, that was practiced in medieval times by monasteries and elite families. In this view, the emergence of the bourgeoisie and the increasing prevalence of commercial relationships signaled a shift in the German tradition of hospitality, as laws that defined the obligation to render hospitality and protect guests (*Gastrecht*) were displaced by laws regulating commerce (*Handelsrecht*) (Koda 2009: 251). Newly tied to commerce, hospitality became more utilitarian. Hans-Dieter Bahr argues that the religious and ethical obligation to open one's door to guests was eclipsed in sixteenth-century Germany by laws that promoted suspicion about the intentions of individuals who crossed borders, that encouraged the monitoring of guests, and that defined guests as strangers (Bahr 1994: 252). Despite the increased emphasis on surveillance, however, in many cities and towns innkeepers were still obligated to offer hospitality as long as they had room, an obligation that included welcoming their guests with a handshake and complimentary beer or wine. When they had no vacancy, innkeepers were obligated to find room in a nearby house or shed where the guests could, at the very least, sleep on a bed of straw (Wallner 1968: 32).

One important caveat: Herr Klaus was paid for the hospitality he extended. While some draw a clear distinction between paid and unpaid hospitality, I follow the lead of those who see more commonalities than differences between them. This perspective is consistent with my definition of hospitality as a sequence of transactions between hosts and guests that are informed by the meanings the two parties attribute to each other and to their interaction.[3] Particular moments in this interaction have the potential to color the two parties' entire experience with each other. Even when the guests pay for the hospitality, then, this moment is only one among many others. While hosts and guests sometimes look to the fact of payment to explain their relationship, the fact that a given episode of hospitality is a paid service does not necessarily constrain the range of meanings that are available to hosts and guests for construing that experience. We should not "limit ourselves to thinking of hospitality as strictly a vehicle for economic exchange and disregard the important social exchanges that persist despite the commercialization of the industry" (Chambers 2000: 11). As R. C. Wood (1994b) writes, "the fact that hospitality is purchased is far less significant than the fact that what is purchased remains undefined beyond a specification of essential terms—for example, bed-and-breakfast, full board and so on" (741). In Austria, some innkeepers offer their guests a "welcome drink" or "greeting drink" *(Begrüßungsgetränk)* to establish rapport (Schrutka-Rechtenstamm 1997a: 472). While the drink is part of the practice of welcoming guests, the hosts emphasize its uncompensated nature, that it is a gift (472). This gift helps to establish a relationship that cannot be characterized as a purely economic transaction (472, 477). In the Greek island of Anafi, some local hosts establish close relationships with guests (Kenna 2010: xvi). "The newly emerged type of 'customer oriented' behavior…attempts to create good-humoured relationships, which might even be defined as 'friendships', and which would engender feelings of personal obligation" (xix). There are, it is true, some cultural contexts where payment would overwhelm the meaning of the transaction of hospitality; the tribal groups Andrew Shryock encountered in Jordan, for example, characterize paid hospitality as dirty work (2004: 41, 47). While such attitudes are the exception rather than the rule, when I provide examples from the literature of hospitality I follow the convention of noting whether or not the hospitality is paid or unpaid for the sake of readers who find this distinction important.

Herr Klaus' Inn and Hospitality in Eastern Germany

On the first morning of my stay, I awoke to a knock on my door. "Hello?" I called out. I heard Herr Klaus respond, "Breakfast's ready." I glanced at my alarm clock; it was only a few seconds from going off.

I emerged from my room into the wide hallway, which was bare except for a lonely chair and a cast-iron lamp dangling from the ceiling. All the doors were closed; I could smell coffee brewing, but I wasn't sure where breakfast was being served. I knocked on the double doors next to my bedroom and to my relief heard Herr Klaus call out, "Come in."

Herr Klaus was sitting on a couch petting a small black dog. The breakfast table was inset with yellow tiles of a type that I had seen at Frau Henneke's apartment the summer before last. The large cabinet with a light wood veneer behind Herr Klaus looked similarly familiar. Hungry for breakfast, I eyed the basket of bread and the tray of sliced cheese. There was also margarine, a stick of butter, and small sealed cups of pork liver pâté and marmalade.

Herr Klaus got up and reached for the coffeepot. I asked for tea instead.
He laughed. "You'd rather have tea. Oh well. Here is the tea selection," he
said, and poured hot water into my glass.

I smiled back at Herr Klaus, equally charmed by the dog now playing
around his feet, an adorable creature with long ears and big droopy eyes.

"It's my daughter's," he said. "She lives in Leipzig, but works in Berlin.
We had breakfast here at 5:30 this morning."

He settled down on his couch and we struck up a conversation. He guessed
that I was a student, and I explained that this was my second visit to Leipzig.
This time, however, I would be here for several months, to do research on how
people were coping with the changes of the last few years.

"My wife and I lived in this apartment for thirty years. She passed away a
year and a half ago." Herr Klaus pointed to a framed photograph of a white-
haired woman on the cabinet shelf on the opposite wall. "And now there is
new construction across the street on what used to be a playground for
children. The women in the neighborhood fought against its closing, but
they lost. The new building is going to block my view of downtown."

Herr Klaus's disclosure of his diminished circumstances added
nuance to our respective roles: a guest-student from the United
States and a local widower-host. He was now no longer merely a
host, but one with a recent history of loss and victimization, and I
was no longer simply a paying guest, but a witness to his suffering. His
wife had died, his neighbors had failed to stop a new building from
encroaching on their community, and his pleasant view would soon be
lost. With the exception of his daughter—who was clearly a source of
hope, as she might still improve her station—he seemed to have few
reasons for optimism. He had many more reasons for self-pity, and his
tone of voice suggested that he knew as much.

In the history of inns and hotels in East Germany, Herr Klaus occupied
a special niche. He and his wife had operated the inn since the 1960s. Back
then, travel and vacations were largely organized by the *Feriendienste*—the
holiday services of large enterprises—and by the trade union, the FDGB.
The *Reisebüro der DDR*, or the GDR travel office, and Inferflug, the state
airline, were also important providers of travel and tourism services (Freyer
2006: 16).[4] I do not know which of these organizations directed guests to
Herr Klaus; I assume that customers came to him through one or more of
these formal channels as well as through an informal local network of
referrals. As a small private business, Herr Klaus's establishment closely
resembled the *Privatquartiere*, enterprises in which individuals rented out

rooms in their houses or apartments. The Klauses' two guest bedrooms could accommodate four people.

In an economy characterized by scarcity, Herr Klaus and his late wife contributed their modest share to the major societal task of providing overnight accommodations. Meeting the demand for accommodations was a challenge that the socialist state took seriously. The right for vacation (*das Recht auf Urlaub*) was anchored in East Germany's constitution. The law obligated the state to build state owned recreation and vacation centers for the working people (Friedrich-Ebert-Stiftung 1985: 8). Eighty percent of East Germans vacationed within the country, with the balance heading to another socialist country in Europe (Freyer 2006: 16).[5] The FDGB was instrumental in meeting this demand; it handled 50 percent of all holiday trips (Görlich 2006–2007: 64). By 1989, the FDGB directly owned 60,000 beds and was responsible for allocating another 71,500 offered by homeowners and hotels (Hachtmann 2007: 144). When demand continued to outstrip supply, the state responded by investing in camping grounds. By 1989, the camping grounds in East Germany could accommodate 400,000 tents (146). Camping gained in popularity as a form of recreation partly because it allowed vacationers to extend their trips beyond the standard two weeks (146).

While the district of Leipzig had all of the above forms of paid hospitality, it was also the setting for high-end hotels that catered to visitors from abroad. These hotels had amenities such as elevators, a telephone in each room, and a concierge. Yet there were only about one thousand hotel beds in Leipzig (Kolinsky 1998: 104). The city needed a large number of beds to host the approximately 650,000 visitors to its spring trade shows, while its fall trade shows regularly drew 300,000 visitors. Most attendees arrived from COMECON-member countries, though the mid-1980s saw more coming from the West, with many arriving by specially scheduled direct trains and flights (Mellor 1991: 143). "Consequently, most visitors during the annual spring and autumn trade fairs had to stay in private rooms in the city" (Kolinsky 1998: 104).

The opportunity to entertain foreign guests was a mark of distinction in East Germany. Innkeepers who represented the country as hosts to foreign guests may have had better access to provisions than ordinary households did. On the other hand, running an inn that brought in guests from abroad also likely required the innkeeper to respond to the perceived security needs of the state by cooperating with the East German secret police, also known as the Stasi. After the peaceful revolution of 1989 (in which Leipzig's residents took a very active part), public opinion condemned those who had enjoyed privileged access to provisions and collaborated with the Stasi under the old order. Travel restrictions had been lifted, and socializing with foreigners was no longer a special privilege.

Herr Klaus was vulnerable to these and other changes wrought by the end of the socialist regime. New hotels, including budget options, soon opened, and individuals traveling to eastern Germany for business suddenly had many attractive choices. "The most dramatic changes in large hotel provision took place between 1994 and 1995 when ten further hotels were opened and the number of bed spaces increased by 69 percent" (Coles 2003: 205). Occupying new or renovated spaces, these new establishments offered superior comforts: rooms that were wide enough to hold queen-sized beds and modern heating. Adequate heating was especially valued between October and May, when the cold weather made guest rooms like Herr Klaus's frigid. The shaft connecting the coal-fed heating unit in the living room to the guest bedroom in which I stayed warmed only a small area by the desk. When I sat down to write in the evenings, I had to wear gloves.

GDR-era establishments such as Herr Klaus's were further undermined by changes in the real estate market that pitted original owners and developers against longtime tenants. Rising property values, the opportunity to charge higher rents, and tax incentives motivated owners to terminate old leases and initiate extensive renovation projects. Longtime residents faced escalating rents, legal challenges, and the prospect of either voluntary relocation or eviction. Herr Klaus's hold on his apartment, in a pre–World War I building with an ornate facade only ten minutes from downtown Leipzig, was tenuous at best.

Even as small inns in old unrenovated buildings were coming under pressure from changes in the market, their economic significance for households such as Herr Klaus's was only increasing. In such households, the spouse who worked outside the home was very likely to have been forced into early retirement—individuals in their late fifties and early sixties, such as Herr Klaus and his wife, were especially vulnerable—and their adult children were also threatened by layoffs. Tens of thousands of Leipzigers lost their jobs in the early 1990s, and many of them were still out of work half a decade later. The unemployment rate, nearly zero under socialism, was 17 percent in Leipzig and twice that in the towns and villages on the periphery of the city. Herr Klaus's daughter commuted to

Berlin for work, and his son drove a taxi. Given the challenges they all faced, the inn was likely a source of comfort for the family. It both generated revenue and provided them with a precious sense of continuity, being a link to a period in their lives in which they had enjoyed a great deal of security and certainty.[6]

PROVISIONING THE GUEST

"You like the bread," he said.

I'd started on my fourth slice. It was heavy whole-wheat bread, and it went well with a thin slice of cheese.

"There's butter. Or do you prefer margarine?"

"Thank you, I'm fine."

"How many slices do you eat?" When I did not answer, he said, "You like your bread dry, without butter or margarine? That's really strange."

This exchange about bread and butter had a didactic subtext: I was being instructed about the boundary or extent of Herr Klaus's hospitality as it applied to food. His practice of bounded hospitality, of giving while withholding, implied that the ideal guest gratefully consumes a moderate amount of the various foods offered to him. This ideal contradicted other ideals of hospitality that I had previously encountered in which the host's task, when guests exhibited a healthy appetite, was to express delight and immediately proceed to offer them more food.

At that moment, however, I was not consciously decoding the meaning of these gestures; I was simply disconcerted by the social distance that Herr Klaus's teasing had created. Seeking to restore the amicable mood that we had sustained until that point, I refrained from removing another slice from the breadbasket and offered Mr. Klaus another arena in which he could assert his authority.

ADVISING AND ADMONISHING THE GUEST

I said, "I'm looking for a place to live in Leipzig for year."

Herr Klaus smiled. "You definitely need to find a place, because you can't stay here for an extended period. I suggest you contact a realtor."

"But wouldn't he charge a lot?"

"One month's rent at the most. How about giving it a try?"

I poured myself another cup of tea.

"The realtor I recommend is Herr Semper." Herr Klaus stirred from the couch and reached for his address book next to the phone. He dialed a number, then greeted the person who picked up at the other end of the line—Herr Semper, presumably.

The ensuing telephone conversation was good-natured, an animated courtesy of gentle teasing. These two must have known each other for a while. When the black dog suddenly barked at his feet, Herr Klaus bent down to pet it, apologizing and laughing profusely. I rather enjoyed the scene. I was becoming a pretext for conversation, part of Leipzig's social glue.

Herr Klaus put down the receiver and handed me a piece of paper with Herr Semper's address. "His office is on Delitzscher Landstrasse. You'll need to take tram number sixteen." He gave me more instructions, which I did not fully understand—but I had a map of Leipzig that I had bought the previous summer and I was confident that I would find Herr Semper's office.

I was glad for this change in tone, though a trace of Herr Klaus's economizing tendency lingered in his statement "You definitely need to find a place, because you can't stay here for an extended period," which reinforced the boundary between us by presuming that I was potentially a drain on his resources. And yet, it was precisely his anxiety that I might overstay my welcome that had stirred him to help me. Indeed, my admission of need was what had shifted the tone of the conversation. I had created some excitement; in place of sadness over his diminished circumstances, of scarcity-driven concern over the number of bread slices that I might eat, was now the prospect of doing a favor for Herr Semper and facilitating a real estate transaction. If Herr Semper could find me an apartment, he would owe Herr Klaus something in return. In a minor way, Herr Klaus would be partaking of the exciting new real estate economy that had emerged since reunification, thereby briefly escaping the cycle of social exclusion.

When I returned to the apartment at 10 o'clock that night, the kitchen counter was bathed in fluorescent light and Herr Klaus was balancing a slice of cheesecake on a wide-bladed knife. He didn't acknowledge me; had he not heard my "hello"? I felt guilty for having stayed out all day without updating him. I tried again: "Good evening," I said.

"Oh, hello. Did you visit Herr Semper?"

"No, I didn't. I got off at the wrong stop."

Herr Klaus stepped into the hallway bearing a slice of cheesecake on a glass plate. Seeing that it was only the first slice of an impressively large confection, I was half-expecting him to offer it to me. Instead, he just said, "But I told you how to get there." Then he repeated his instructions from this morning. "I even called Herr Semper on your behalf. You can't stay here forever. But now, this is your problem." I opened my mouth to speak, but he cut me off, repeating loudly, "Now this is your problem. This is your problem."

Turning toward the living room door, he announced, "You should have taken a taxi."

Herr Klaus expressed hostility by refusing to fully reciprocate my greeting and preventing me from explaining why I did not find Herr Semper. He then cut off the prospect of his offering me future help with the phrase *Jetzt, das ist deine Problem*—"Now this is your problem." Repeating this sentence in a derisive tone, he made it impossible for me to reestablish an amicable atmosphere. His use of the familiar second-person pronoun (*deine*) rather than the polite formal form (*Ihre*) was meant to belittle me. He was chiding me for not following his instructions and for not taking a taxi when I failed to reach Herr Semper's by tram.

Herr Klaus's didactic streak had been in evidence from my very first morning at the inn. At that time he was mostly advising and informing, sharing his knowledge with me in a manner that built rapport, a rapport that had deepened when he confided his woes. His didactic tendency was also woven into his constant economizing, a pattern that became evident when he instructed me on the limits of his generosity: I should moderate my intake of bread, I should not overstay. And now it seemed as though I had transgressed another kind of limit, perhaps irrevocably.

Herr Klaus remained largely hostile to me for the duration of my stay, and I learned to respect his boundaries and limitations. After all, he was an aging widower, vulnerable to declining health and fortunes, who was extending hospitality to me within the confines of a modest apartment. There were only two later occasions on which we temporarily repaired our relationship. Both of these episodes, interestingly, were associated with short-lived improvements in his perceived status.

I was alone at the breakfast table, but the acrid smell of Herr Klaus's cigarettes hung in the room. As I was finishing my meal, he walked in. "Tonight the clock is moving back one hour," he announced. "I'm telling you this so that you know I've had an extra hour of sleep."

I wasn't sure what to make of this information, but I acknowledged him politely as I poured more hot water into my glass mug. His deliberate tone suggested a well-developed sense of discipline. It seems that he would not have

granted himself an extra hour of sleep if it were not for the imminent changing of the clocks.
"You can have a new tea bag if you want."
It was a peace overture. I suddenly felt more optimistic about my day.
"No, it's okay."
"I've no understanding for tea." He smiled knowingly. "I only drink coffee."
Attending to what I thought he implied, I said, "Only strong coffee?"
He beamed. "Yes. Strong coffee."

THE HOST'S SUPERIORITY ACROSS CULTURES

Following a perfunctory exchange about the return to standard time, Herr Klaus had signaled a willingness to relieve some of the tension between us by offering me another teabag. But instead of responding enthusiastically to this cue, I declined his offer of a teabag. I wanted to signal self-sufficiency. Yet even as I did so, I realized that he might interpret my response as a rejection of his peace offering. To correct this impression, I seized on the gendered subtext of tea and coffee and provisionally attributed to Herr Klaus an exclusive preference for the latter. He interpreted my statement as the compliment that I meant it to be, confirming his attachment to strong coffee and accentuating its masculine connotation by repeating the word *strong*. This brief suspension of hostilities was predicated on Herr Klaus's gaining the upper hand.

The presumed superiority of the host is an important subtext in the practice of hospitality in various cultures. Fredrik Barth (1981) writes that poor Pashtun farmers extend hospitality to strangers in a manner that sustains their "self-esteem...in the face of the wealth and luxury of neighboring Oriental civilizations," civilizations which they nonetheless believe to have inferior ethical premises (107). Foreign guests, Barth explains, "are made to recognize the sovereignty of local people" (107). Writing about hospitality in Crete, Michael Herzfeld emphasizes the local hosts' tendency to transcend structural inequalities by rewarding, rather than punishing, their more privileged guests. Hosts, he argues, do not enact "Turnerian social dramas" but rather "rites of inversion" that turn "perceived" inequalities on their "head through irony or even generosity (as in acts of hospitality)" (Herzfeld 2000: 233). He defines the act of hospitality as the inclusion, incorporation, and subordination of the guest to the host (1987: 77). "By inviting a Turk (or any foreigner) into one's home, one simultaneously incorporates the potentially dangerous representative of a feared foreign power and expresses pride in the national virtue of hospitality" (84). Aida Kanafani's account of hospitality in the United Arab Emirates is an important precedent.

> The guest, she explains, is a potential evildoer precisely because of his ambiguity. He enters a new realm and until assimilated he remains a stranger. Even close relatives also remain symbolically strangers till incorporated. Both the host and the guest share in a series of rites of incorporation geared toward the reduction of the antagonism, beginning with food consumption and ending with perfuming and incensing.[7]

The host minimizes "the guest's power" by managing the variety, quantity, and quality of the "food and body rituals," subtleties that the guest knows to interpret as an ongoing commentary about his or her relationship with the host (100).

Perceived superiority—this time associated with geopolitical differences, worldly experience, and the social prestige associated with heterosexual masculinity—was an important subtext in another interaction that I shared with Herr Klaus and a couple from western Germany. On this occasion, Herr Klaus again conveyed his knowledge to his guests, but he did so in a pleasant way that drew everyone together even as it elevated his own status.

There was a couple at the breakfast table, a man and a woman. Herr Klaus was in a chatty mood. His regional vernacular—a local variant of the Saxon dialect—contrasted with the couple's speech, which sounded more like standard, "unmarked" High German. Leipzig, he explained to them, drew foreign visitors thanks to its fall and spring trade shows, and he had been hosting foreign guests in his apartment for the past thirty years.

The woman smiled, revealing a perfect set of teeth.

Herr Klaus continued, "You noticed the Intercontinental Hotel between this neighborhood and downtown? Nord Street used to have quite a reputation. There were prostitutes just down the street."

The couple was impressed by this inside information. The man, who was wearing a fashionable blazer, acknowledged that "East Germany was not what we in the West think it was."

This remark assured Herr Klaus that the knowledge he was sharing was seen as important and valuable. When the couple left, he stood up and exclaimed, "Rupiti!" I had no idea what this meant, but it sounded like the happy chirp of a bird.

"Is that Italian?" I asked.

"No, Russian. I need to prepare more beds. This is a mini-hotel."

In his conversation with his western German guests, Herr Klaus took on the role of someone imparting privileged local knowledge, informing his guests of how things *really* were in East Germany. He conjured the image of prostitutes catering to foreign guests as an aspect of East Germany that few westerners know about, and the male guest gracefully conceded that he was ignorant of this phenomenon, implicitly acknowledging that he had not been part of this sexual traffic and setting himself out as less experienced—and perhaps less manly—than the worldly-wise innkeeper. Soon thereafter, the male guest advanced a related idea when he proposed that western Germans are at fault for falsely thinking they know eastern Germany. The guest was ingratiating himself with Herr Klaus by acknowledging his compatriots' ignorance of the East German experience, even as he also adeptly distanced himself from the stereotype of "the Besser Wessi who knows the east German situation much better than the east Germans themselves do... " (De Soto 2000: 77).

One might speculate that the western German guest sacrificed his group's status to avert some minor punishment or humiliation that he sensed might otherwise be coming to him and his wife. He may also have accepted this momentary humiliation as an unavoidable part of the experience of being a western German guest in a small apartment-based pension in eastern Germany. Anthropologists have recognized that such minor rites of sacrifice, punishment, and reward can "imbue places and events with identities that best represent... particular interests and values" (Chambers 2000: 31). Working in Buenos Aires, Katherine Hite described the unpleasant demeanor of the guide at Esma, the former Navy Mechanical School that had once been a detention and torture center and is now a museum commemorating the human rights violations in Argentina during the military dictatorship of the 1970s and early 1980s. Since the visitors were American, the guide's unpleasant demeanor could be interpreted as a symbolic retaliation for the United States' alleged complicity in past human rights violations in Argentina (Hite 2015: 44). Regardless of her motive, her harsh manner communicated the true meaning of this place to the foreigners, and in that sense provided a more authentic experience for the visitors (44).

After the couple left the breakfast table, Herr Klaus declared optimistically that his inn was a "mini-hotel." His punctuating that optimism with an exclamation in Russian was both suggestive and poignant, given the rapidly diminishing importance of the Russian language in eastern Germany at the time. By the mid-1990s, English, French, Italian, or Spanish would have seemed more fitting idioms for playful borrowings like this one.

Herr Klaus's burst of optimism had occasioned a fleeting moment of cordiality between us. Most of our other interaction, however, remained unpleasant. After I declared my intention to set another appointment with the realtor, Herr Klaus said only, "Das ist deine Entscheidung." "This is your decision. Remember, I can extend your stay here only by a day or two, not more. This is your problem now. You must decide. You must decide." He repeated this last phrase, *Du musst entscheiden*, as though singing a refrain.[8]

Downward Mobility and Hostility

A few days later, I finally met Herr Semper. He drove a wide-bodied blue sedan with an exceptionally smooth ride, which cushioned us as we rode over the construction debris and steel plates that covered sections of the road. His western German car was a sign that he was one of those reaping the benefits of the economic restructuring. I breathed in the fragrance of leather in his car, glad to be on my way to finding a more permanent home in Leipzig.

The next day, I told Herr Klaus that I planned to take the apartment that Herr Semper had shown me, and he promptly offered to call Herr Semper on my behalf. But after asking Herr Semper's wife when her husband would be back in the office, the message he gave to her to convey was: "I don't know whether the young man wants to take the apartment or not."

I was annoyed at this misrepresentation, but I kept quiet. When he got off the phone, he said, "I would let you stay one night longer than planned, but not more. As far as I'm concerned you might as well be living on the street. It's up to you. You must decide." Then he repeated this last phrase in a singing tone: "Du musst entscheiden."

Herr Klaus had deliberately distorted the message that I had been eager to convey to Herr Semper. Rather than announce that I would take the apartment her husband had shown me, Herr Klaus told Frau Semper that he "did not know" whether or not I wanted the apartment. Why did he do this? There are at least two goals that Herr Klaus might have had in mind. First, it is possible that by deliberately misreporting my intentions, he felt that he was actually giving Herr Semper, the realtor, a more plausible, neutral forecast of my future actions. He may have suspected that I was pursuing another apartment or rooming situation on the side, though this was not the case. Second, by communicating ignorance of my true intentions, the inn-keeper was implicitly saying that he was not responsible for the success of the realtor's efforts to find me an apartment. In signaling to Herr Semper that I might prove to be a disappointment, Herr Klaus may have been seeking to avoid blame should Herr Semper complain to him that I had backed out of the transaction—while at the same time, and even more importantly, refuting any accusation that he could not tell the difference between a serious prospect and a flighty young man.

From this perspective, we may view the phone call as intended to repair Herr Klaus's reputation with Herr Semper. It is important to remember that the two men's circumstances were starkly different: Herr Klaus was running a two-bedroom pension on the third floor of an old building with a coal-fired heating system, while Semper had a real estate office in a rapidly developing northern suburb of Leipzig. Younger than Herr Klaus by fifteen years, he was far more likely to profit from the influx of investment from western Germany that was fueling the real estate market in and around the city. The economic disparity between the two men rendered Herr Klaus vulnerable to the charge that he was not up to the challenge of holding on, let alone succeeding, in the post-socialist era.

While Herr Klaus's conversation with Frau Semper may have been meant to repair his standing with her husband, his somewhat hostile comments immediately after the phone call seemed intended to exact punishment on me—for my failure to reach Herr Semper the first time, which had put him in a bad light and may well have reminded him of his inferior socioeconomic circumstances—and, simultaneously, to shore up his own self-esteem.[9] He accomplished these two closely related goals by telling me again that it would be *my* decision to take the apartment or not, thus framing his intervention as a purposeful distortion of the message I had intended to convey to the realtor. To emphasize further that his intention was punitive, he underplayed the housing options that were actually available to me—there were several inns and hotels in the city, and the tourist office had capable and helpful staff—and said that he would not care if I were rendered homeless. Yet at the same time, he offered to let me stay one extra night if I needed to. While the skewed balance that Herr Klaus struck between rewards and punishments was not to my liking, I was grateful that he would let me stay one more day than I had planned, which meant that I would not need to move to another inn or hotel to bridge the gap between the original departure date and the start of my lease.

LOYALTY TO LOCAL AUTHORITIES

Herr Klaus maintained the social distance that he had put between us. On the morning of my last day at the inn, he greeted me with a reproach. "You're late for breakfast," he said. I sat down and looked at my watch. It was 9:06 a.m. Strictly speaking, Herr Klaus was right.

"This is your last meal," he said.

Was this a joke, or a verdict? I remembered all the previous occasions when he had berated me, and felt no urge to smile.

"Do you know the derivation of the expression 'last meal'?" he continued. "It refers to the last meal served to a prisoner before he's executed."

Herr Klaus's joke was really a fantasy, a parallel reality in which the inn was a prison, and I was his prisoner. Styling himself as the prison's warden, Herr Klaus was now informing the prisoner of his fate—a symbolic execution—and thereby completing a sequence of exchanges in which the innkeeper successively informs, advises, and reprimands the guest. From now on, it followed, he would no longer advise me. In making his morbid joke, he had symbolically discharged his obligation to inform and correct. The gesture also promised an imminent end to his need to economize. The guest's "execution" would remove the threat that the guest posed to the innkeeper's resources, relieving the host of the task of preventing the guest from consuming more than his fair share.

At the same time, Herr Klaus's joke revealed another interesting aspect of his role as host: an allegiance to local authorities. Innkeepers and hoteliers in Germany are required to collect certain basic information about their guests—their names and the citizenship information found in their passports—and to provide this information to the local authorities.[10] This information can be helpful to hosts in the event that their guests fail to pay or steal from them, and it can also benefit guests in case of an emergency. Yet in making his joke, Herr Klaus was not conjuring the image of local authorities assisting guests, but rather pointing to the authorities' punitive powers.

Ironically, Herr Klaus's fantasy of the guest as prisoner actually cast his own hospitality in a more generous light. Prisoners who have been sentenced to death can be sustained by their jailers at minimal expense: mere food and water until the day of execution. Herr Klaus's hospitality, by implicit contrast, certainly exceeded the minimum required to sustain me. Moreover, an act of "hospitality" to a prisoner facing execution has an unreciprocated, altruistic quality, because this "guest" will never be a return visitor, let alone a source of referrals. The surplus generosity and consequent sacrifice therefore elevated Herr Klaus's hospitality, which now could be seen as a gift offered without expectation of reward.

Of course, Herr Klaus's joke also had a more petty aim: to belittle his guest and aggrandize himself. The innkeeper's desire to be seen as strong is understandable, considering his stressful life circumstances. The government had torn apart the safety net that older East Germans of Herr Klaus's generation had expected to be able to rely on when they retired or if their health failed. Instead, as they approached retirement, Herr Klaus and his cohort were confronting unemployment, rising living costs, and diminished expectations, as well as a new cadre of local and state authorities who were aggressively enforcing a complex restitution process aimed at compensating individuals for property confiscated by the communists or the Nazis. This restitution process often led to evictions. Calling up the image of a strong state authority that could decide an individual's fate thus spoke to the innkeeper's need for safety and security, a need that the current regime was failing to meet. The fantasy likely also gave him a temporary feeling of empowerment relative to those among his guests whose own prosperity was aligned with the policies that were changing his life for the worse. Momentarily assuming the guise of a punitive authority figure allowed the host to temporarily imagine me, a young student from a wealthy Western society whose very identity accentuated the host's predicament, as powerless and weak.

Lastly, the image of the guest as a prisoner mirrored the host's own difficult circumstances, carrying intimations of a future in which he would no longer be able to extend any hospitality whatsoever. Having lost his wife a year and half ago, Herr Klaus was now burdened with all the tasks of running his household and inn. He washed sheets and towels, shopped for provisions and prepared breakfast, aired and cleaned the two guest rooms, coordinated guests' arrivals and departures, and collected the nightly fee of fifty marks (thirty-five U.S. dollars). These activities must have been physically challenging for a heavyset man in his mid-sixties who smoked heavily. He may also have felt emotionally burdened by these chores, now that his wife was gone.

The Three Values that Inform the Innkeeper's Practice of Hospitality

While I do not know how the innkeeper and his late wife interacted with their guests when she was alive, I see a link between his outbursts of hostility and the particular exchanges that appear to have brought his frustration and anger to the surface. My seemingly untempered appetite for bread was a source of concern for him, as it suggested that I lacked an awareness of the proper balance between what a host is offering the guest and what the guest should consume, offending his sense of fairness. My later failure to find Herr Semper exacerbated Herr Klaus's sense of vulnerability, eliciting a pedantic response: he chastised me, looking to teach me a lesson. He reverted to being more sociable when business seemed to pick up, but this was only a brief respite. When he exclaimed in enthusiasm about his additional guests, he did so in Russian, harking back to his East German socialization and implicitly underscoring the challenges he faced as he attempted to adjust to a new marketplace dominated by western German investors. Even after I succeeded in meeting Herr Semper, the rift between us remained unhealed, and the innkeeper's pedantic outbursts were now always laced with hostility. His reluctance to allow me to stay an extra day made it seem as though such an extension had challenged his frugal sensibility. All this culminated in a morbid joke that invoked a multivalent fantasy: on the surface, the fantasy was that I would be executed, but at a deeper level, it was about the innkeeper's prescribed, though increasingly vexed, allegiance to the punitive function of government authority. While government-supported economic transformations were putting his inn and his livelihood at risk, the fantasy cast him in a supporting role in relation to government authority.

When, years later, I began to read through the history of hospitality in Germany, I was surprised to find hosts who lived in very different times and circumstances expressing the same three primary values that I saw embodied in Herr Klaus's behavior toward me: provisioning guests appropriately, offering them astute advice, remaining loyal to local authorities. The historical record suggests remarkable continuity in these values. What is more variable is whether, when a given host acts on these values, he is doing so to reward his guests or to punish them.[11] Indeed, what is particularly interesting about Herr Klaus's case is how it demonstrates that the underlying values of hospitality among innkeepers in Germany can accommodate sharply opposing social outcomes: both drawing closer to one's guests and distancing oneself from them.

THE HISTORY OF HOSPITALITY IN GERMANY

The values I encountered in the person of Herr Klaus resonate across the history of paid hospitality in Germany.[12] Economizing, instructing one's guests, and showing one's allegiance to governing authorities all feature prominently in this history.

According to the earliest extant historical records, travelers in German lands enjoyed a right to hospitality *(Gastrecht)* that obligated house-holders and landlords to offer accommodations and food free of charge. Classical sources on the German peoples, such as Caesar's *Gallic Wars* and Tacitus's *Germania*, indicate that among the Germans, strangers looking for a place to stay would first offer a gift to their hosts, upon the acceptance of which they were entitled to lodging for up to three days—a time limit that protected the hosts from guests who might abuse their right to hospitality (Wallner 1968: 14). A German proverb, one which is still heard today, recalls this ancient three-day limit while also conveying an econo-mizing sensibility: "Den ersten Tag ein Gast, den zweiten eine Last, den dritten stinkt er fast" (on the first day, he's a guest; on the second, he's a burden; on the third, he stinks) (Wallner 1968: 14). There are several related sayings that warn against guests who might abuse one's hospitality, such as "Gast und Fisch stinken nach drei Tagen" (guests and fish stink after three days) and "Dreier Tage Gast—allen eine Last" (three days a guest—to everyone a burden) (Schrutka-Rechtenstamm 1997b: 48). This three-day limit apparently had some currency in England as well: the sixteenth-century English dramatist John Lyly asserted that "after three days, fish and guests stink" (Dikeç, Clark and Barnett 2009: 5).

The three-day rule is also associated with a pedantic tendency, with hosts reminding guests that it is time for them to leave. In his lexicon of German proverbs, Lutz Roehrich records that hosts would send their guests a not-so-subtle hint by asking them, "Why did Christ lie in the grave for three days and then rise?" (Schrutka-Rechtenstamm 1997b: 48). This strictness has been, at times, reflected in German law; in German lands in the early Roman times, for example, hosts became legally respon-sible for their guests' conduct starting on the fourth day (Wallner 1968: 63). Being liable for their guests' conduct likely also reinforced hosts' economizing sensibility—as any misconduct by guests could lead to their hosts having to pay restitution—and motivated hosts to apprise their guests of local norms.

German innkeepers were also expected to keep the interests of the governing authorities in mind when they extended hospitality. Many guests, especially traveling merchants, played important economic roles, and the authorities fixed the prices that could be charged for a night's stay to ensure fairness. In one documented case from 1530, guests' complaints about unfair pricing led to more regulations (Wallner 1968: 32). On the other hand, not all guests were welcomed. In medieval times, *Utlude*, or near-strangers who lived in a city's surrounding areas, did not have the right to stay overnight in cities during trade fairs, because city merchants feared competition from them (Koda 2009: 244–245). In the tenth century, authorities sometimes gave permission for people to open a tavern in exchange for the right to collect fees from the operation. Some of these taverns also served overnight guests (Wallner 1968: 25). A license to operate a guesthouse carried with it the right to hang a sign announcing the establishment, a privilege known as *Schildgerechtigkeit* (Wallner 1968: 31). In central and northern Germany, the function of innkeeper was associated with judicial officials. In Leipzig, the mayor was also a pub owner (Wallner 1968: 31).[13] By the end of the seventeenth century, innkeepers in Leipzig were required to keep records of their guests' names, whether they were domestic or foreign, where they came from, their occupations, the number of people and horses that were with them, and how long they were planning to stay (Bahr 1994: 255).

These cultural resonances extend to modern-day Germany. In a humorous advice book about hospitality from the 1950s, the author, whose ancestors had socialized in the courts of the nobility (Kardorff 1958: 7), instructs her western German audience on how one can entertain without spending much money. Her first chapter, "Do Guests Cost Money?" (22), discusses ways of serving food that is tasty yet cheap (24). The context of this book, of course, was the extreme economic deprivation following World War II, which affected Germans of all classes, including once well-to-do families. A more recent example is the play *The Golden Dragon* (*Der Goldene Drache*), by Roland Schimmelpfennig, which depicts a storeowner and his female houseguest. The storeowner is attracted to the guest, a foreigner who dreams of becoming a dancer, yet at the same time is repelled by her economic insecurity and her dependence on him for room and board. The drama is set in his well-stocked apartment above the store. The storeowner likens himself to a hardworking ant and his guest to a carefree grasshopper, citing the familiar parable to underscore the value of economizing. Meanwhile, his pedantic outbursts rehearse the traditional German value of advising and informing one's guests. Eventually, the storeowner turns himself into a warden, holding his guest captive in his apartment against her will. Because she is a foreigner without legal status in Germany, he exudes the confidence of one who knows he is on the right side of the law, rhetorically aligning himself with local authorities (Studio Theater, Washington, D.C., November 3, 2011).

As demonstrated by the previous examples, I recognize three distinct value orientations persisting across greatly varied times and places in the history of hospitality in Germany: fairly providing for one's guests, informing and advising one's guests, and aligning oneself with the local authorities. My specific interaction with Herr Klaus, and his stressed circumstances as a manager of a small establishment in post-socialist Leipzig, help explain the specific mix of rewards and punishments that he meted out to me. The innkeeper did not see himself as stepping out of his role as a host when he punished his guest; he could do so while remaining true to his core values of hospitality. The flexibility of his core values meant that he could define an interaction in which he vented his anger and frustration at his guest as falling within the scope of his profession's practice of hospitality.

EXAMPLES OF HOSPITALITY AND HOSTILITY ACROSS CULTURES

In inns and hotels around the world, owners, managers, and employees engage in both rewarding and punishing their guests. While scholars have tended to focus on the practice of rewarding guests, they have also recognized that hosts have a need to warn guests that they should not misbehave and to signal that, if the guests cross certain boundaries, they will face retaliation or punishment. According to one such account, Scottish innkeepers seeking to prevent situations that might give rise to conflict, such as inappropriate sexual conduct, hang humorous signs to remind guests of the rules of etiquette and decorate their inns with family pictures and religious symbols to reinforce the message that propriety is taken seriously (Di Domenico and Fleming 2009: 257–263). Such mechanisms define the inn as a home that is "a domestic retreat, a normalized family space" (249). If these social cues fail to have the desired effect, Scottish innkeepers may confront their guests face to face. One innkeeper described his style of admonishing offending guests as "polite but firm" (260). Similarly, in New Zealand, "hosts' relationship with their commercial home can be summarized in the aphorism 'my home is my castle,' which reveals itself through an underlying sense of defiance in terms of the respondents' attitudes to the outside world and in particular commercial homestay hosting" (McIntosh, Lynch, and Sweeney et al. 2011: 517).

R. C. Wood (1994a) argues that hotel culture constrains behavior for the purpose of ensuring "harmony and the maintenance of decorum" (78). Rachel Sherman (2005) goes a step further: while Wood emphasizes the harmony in the host-guest exchange, Sherman emphasizes potential sources of conflict. She describes how employees of a luxury hotel on the West Coast of the United States harness "a sense of exclusivity" (149) to assert their self-worth. They punish guests (and each other) to protect themselves "from acknowledging their own subordination" (149). According to Sherman, "the characteristics of luxury (prestige, expense, intimate knowledge of guests, and so on) laid the foundation for strategies of status, condescension, and critique" (149). When colleagues and guests fail to affirm the employees' status claims, "overt conflict (among workers) and small punishments (toward guests) are often the result" (153). Knowledge of guests' past behavior can inform specific acts of condescension toward them. For example, modeling how an employee might respond to a demanding guest whose requests for help with the Internet on past visits to the hotel have annoyed the staff, an assistant manager suggests striking a patronizing tone: "Are you sure you checked all your connections, Mr. D'Angelo?" (144). The guest might ignore the tone of condescension, or take offense at it, or not detect it all. Here, R. C. Wood's comment that hotel culture aims to ensure "harmony and the maintenance of decorum" (1994a: 78) is instructive: I suspect that the luxury hotel employees Sherman observed were purposely meting out minor reprimands that were just small enough not to provoke guests to retaliate and thereby disrupt the hotel's decorous ambience.

The fact that Herr Klaus could upbraid and punish his guest for a period of days while remaining true to the values of being a host is noteworthy. Have German innkeepers always enjoyed the same flexibility? If so, perhaps this very flexibility explains the resilience of these values, persisting as they have throughout the history of hospitality in Germany. And if that is true, then we might hypothesize that hosts in other societies who conform to institutional variants of hospitality that prescribe a narrower, more generous repertoire of behavior could find themselves under strain when economic or other circumstances make such behavior less tenable. To put it more bluntly, hosts who are obligated to be always generous and pleasing toward their guests may eventually be compelled by circumstances to withdraw their hospitality altogether.

While more evidence would be needed to substantiate this hypothesis, some research does suggest that a constricted repertoire of values is associated with abrupt changes in hospitality practices. Charles Lindholm, who did fieldwork among the Pashtuns in the Swat Valley of northern Pakistan, writes that the site of hospitality in that society has shifted from the neighborhood *hujera*, or men's house, to guest rooms owned by "middle-level khans" and "successful laborers and herdsmen" (Lindholm 1982: 229). But traditionally, indeed "within recent memory, all guests were put up and fed at the neighborhood *hujera* at the expense of the local khan. The whole neighborhood would contribute to the care and feeding of the guest in a display of communal help" (228).[14] In some cases, social and economic changes compel would-be hosts to refrain from offering hospitality at all. Writing about Odessa and Batumi, in Georgia, Abel Polese notes that "a fast economic transition is urging a number of people to renegotiate the complex rituals linked with hospitality" (2009: 77) [*sic*].[15] Similarly, in response to extreme economic hardship in post-soviet Kyrgyzstan, "many Kyrgyz had stopped visiting their relatives because of social reciprocity norms, which required them to return the favor whenever their relatives accommodated them" (Kuehnast 2000: 113). Kathleen Kuehnast notes that "in a culture where accommodating a guest is nearly an art form, the curtailment of hospitality to their relatives and friends was seen as a great personal shame among many of my informants" (113).

HOSTILITY AND RESILIENT FORMS OF HOSPITALITY

The long history in Germany of the values I have identified suggests that Herr Klaus was practicing a culturally resilient form of hospitality. Other forms of hospitality around the world have not so easily endured, despite often being revered in their local cultures. Anthropological research suggests that the forms of hospitality that are the most cherished entail values that restrict hosts to serving and pleasing their guests. Yet as we have learned, these standards can be hard to sustain when social circumstances change. Meanwhile, forms of hospitality that allow hosts a broader spectrum of behavior, from befriending their guests to upbraiding them, are less often seen as templates of ideal conduct, yet may have a greater chance of persisting.[16]

Herr Klaus practiced the latter kind of hospitality, a variant that resonates with the writings of Emile Benveniste and Jacques Derrida on this topic. Benveniste found that the root word for "hospitality" (in Latin, English, and German, among other European languages) refers to both friends and enemies (Friese 2010: 324; see also McNulty 2007: ix–xii). Derrida, meanwhile, advanced the concept of "hostipitality," the notion that hospitality is "inconceivable without hostility, and vice versa" (Arpaci 2008: 162). Derrida argued that hospitality presupposes borders between "familial and the non-familial," "foreign and the non-foreign," "citizen and non-citizen" (Derrida and Dufourmantelle 2000: 49). He conceived of an ideal of hospitality in which hosts accept strangers without asking them anything, even their names (Friese 2003: 9). The notional guest whom this ideal conjures recalls Simmel's idea of the stranger as a nameless generalized other rather than a unique individual (11). Derrida juxtaposed this ideal of unconditional hospitality—which he calls "absolute" hospitality—with forms of hospitality that are grounded in political and practical concerns (Derrida and Dufourmantelle 2000: 29).

Ideals of hospitality offer insight into the scope and depth of human cooperation and sociability. As he explores the deeper meaning of the offering of hospitality, Karl Wernhart (1997) draws on the philosopher Hans-Dieter Bahr, author of *Die Sprache des Gastes: Eine Metaethik* (*The Language of the Guest: A Metaethic*, 1994). According to Bahr, the tradition of allowing prisoners condemned to death to choose their last meal is proof that social relations trump legal formalities (Hans-Dieter Bahr in Wernhart 1997: 28). The fact that even the condemned may be treated as guests underscores an underlying ethic of sociability.

Some social scientists have drawn on Bahr's and (more commonly) Derrida's writings on hospitality, including the latter's ideal of absolute hospitality, to describe the treatment of refugees, immigrants, and other marginalized groups. They cast marginalized individuals as guests and locals and representatives of the state as hosts (Molz and Gibson 2007; Hamington 2010). Ramona Lenz uses such a framework to investigate the plight of refugees detained in a hotel in Crete (2010: 216–221): In her account, the refugees are the guests and the guards watching the asylum seekers play the role of hosts. The questions she asks in her research—"who is welcome as a guest and who is not?", who has the resources "to act as a host and who has not"? (2010: 211)—are partly inspired by Derrida's interest in hospitality as a gateway to understanding state sovereignty and the constitution of self and other.[17]

Another important source for scholars of sovereignty and individual rights is Emmanuel Kant's writings on hospitality. Kant envisioned "a single globally recognized set of laws of hospitality which would guarantee the security of those moving across nation-state borders" (Dikeç, Clark and Barnett 2009: 5; see also Melville 2007: 39–40). Seyla Benhabib draws on Kant to define hospitality as consisting of "all human rights claims that are cross-border in scope" (2005: 90). She notes that "the modern state system is caught between sovereignty and hospitality, between the prerogative to choose to be a party to cosmopolitan norms and human rights treaties, and the obligation to extend recognition of these human rights to all" (90).

Interestingly, the mining the metaphorical meanings of hospitality, guest and host to illuminate legally and politically grounded processes of marginalization and exclusion has drawn some criticism. Mustafa Dikeç and his coauthors have asserted that "the translation of hospitality into a principle of critical analysis is neither unproblematic nor necessary" (2009: 4). Dikeç, along with other scholars from the humanities and social sciences, participated in a workshop entitled "Giving Space, Taking Time: A Workshop on Hospitality and Generosity" and contributed to an issue of *Paragraph: A Journal of Modern Critical Theory* that was entirely dedicated to the subject of hospitality (13). In their introduction to this issue, Dikeç and his two coauthors explain that their aim was to "engage with the 'proximities' that provoke acts of hospitality and inhospitality more carefully—to attend more closely to their spatial and temporal dimensions and to the relational qualities of identity, community and placement" (4).

In this part of the book, I have followed the more cautious approach outlined by Dikeç et al, acknowledging their basic insight that hospitality includes "acts of hospitality and inhospitality" alike (4). I have recounted my relations with Herr Klaus, and our mutual guest-host interaction, one incident at a time. This approach, I believe, has allowed me to show how even a hostile interaction can be interpreted by a host as being an ideal expression of hospitality, as long as the host believes that the hospitality he has offered exceeds what his guests actually deserve.

ANTHROPOLOGY AND THE REPRESENTATION OF HOSTILITY

I hope that after reading the first part of this book, my readers will not mistake it for a long complaint letter: a Western traveler comes to the former East Germany, encounters a grumpy host, and is so insulted by the poor customer service he receives that he decides to write an angry book about his experience. This was not my aim. Rather, I have presented the story of my interaction with Herr Klaus to illustrate the counter-intuitive idea that hostility can be an integral component of hospitality. I have uncovered the values that informed Herr Klaus's practice—economizing, advising his guests, and allying himself with local authorities—and suggested that these values can be traced back over the long history of hospitality in Germany. And drawing on this history and my readings in cultural anthropology, I have argued that traditions of hospitality that accommodate conflict and aggression may be more resilient than traditions that restrict hosts to serving, befriending, and protecting their guests.

As became clear to me over the course of my stay at his inn, my host in Leipzig saw himself as someone weathering difficult life circumstances with grace. Nonetheless, the impression that he has left in these pages is predominantly a negative one—and for an anthropologist who is loathe to damage the reputations of the individuals and communities who have hosted him, this raises a big problem. Anthropologists should always be aware of the power imbalances between themselves and their hosts, and of the ways in which negative stereotypes perpetuate injustice at different levels (both individual and societal). But while I realize that my characterization of an ill-humored Herr Klaus might erode his standing and that of other people who are in similar circumstances, I believe that my observations of his abrasive demeanor are essential evidence for my argument: that the values on which Herr Klaus's practice of hospitality was based allow hosts a strikingly wide range of behavior, a range that comfortably accommodates confronting and upbraiding one's guests.

Reflections on Fieldwork, Other Social Institutions, and *Bildung*

I hope, too, that the first part of this work will inspire further thought. Like all case studies, this one leaves us with as many questions as answers. Among the questions that arose in the back of my mind were these: what is the relationship between cultural anthropology and hospitality? Is my argument about the scope of behavior and resilience relevant to other social institutions, such as parenting, education, healthcare or the workplace? Does this case study shed light on German culture as a whole?

Let me briefly address these three questions here, if only as an inducement to future research.

What is the relationship between hospitality and cultural anthropology? To follow Michale Herzfeld, "ultimately, all ethnographers, even those who are considered native in any sense, are guests" (2000: 233). Anthropologists are often obliged to secure hospitality in the course of their fieldwork, and in the process, their hosts often become their research partners or subjects (informants). Indeed, one of the preconditions for successful fieldwork is the anthropologist's ability to reframe the hospitality that he or she receives in the society under study. There are many obstacles. When local people shun an anthropologist out of suspicion that he or she is not merely a traveling stranger, whom one could invite to one's home or otherwise welcome as a guest, but also an agent of some feared institution, such as the police or an intelligence service, the anthropologist must work to change this perception. Sometimes people confuse anthropologists with tourists, a label from which many anthropologists are at pains to dissociate themselves (Crick 1989: 311). For their part, anthropologists typically recast their hosts as informants and research subjects who are located at a particular social and cultural nexus—a reframing which sanctions the anthropologists' redeployment of the hospitality that is extended to them in the service of their professional enterprise (Colson 1989: 3; Ladner 2014: 126). This double effort to solicit hospitality while turning key hosts into informants predisposes many anthropologists to idealize hospitality and thereby avoid confronting the implications of Benveniste and Derrida's core insight that conflict and hostility are integral aspects of hospitality. Moreover, to repay their informants for the valuable insights they have provided, anthropologists often feel an obligation to praise their qualities as hosts. This perceived obligation to safeguard the host community's reputation further deters anthropologists from exploring the hostility that is sometimes a dimension of hospitality.

Could the distinctions that I draw between different forms of hospitality—between the variants that accommodate conflict and the variants that do not—apply to other social institutions as well? Since my readers' interests likely extend well beyond hospitality, this question is worth posing. I can imagine asking it with regard to institutions such as parenthood, education, healthcare, and the workplace. Both across and within cultures, each of these institutions has its own specific set of values. It would be worth investigating whether institutional forms founded on values that accommodate a broad range of behavior (from cooperation and love to aggression and retaliation) are more resilient than other forms that restrict their participants' repertoire of behavior to cooperating and rewarding with each other. To do so, we would need to examine the complementary roles that form the basis of each institution. For example, to examine different models of parenting, we would have to look at the values that inform parent–child interaction. For education, we would examine student–teacher interaction; for healthcare, caregiver-patient interaction; and for the workplace, employer–employee interaction.[18]

Lastly, the first part of this book may also have something more to tell us about the city of Leipzig and, more broadly, about German culture and society. I have already discussed Herr Klaus's immediate circumstances, the hospitality industry in eastern Germany, and the history of hospitality in Germany. I wonder, though, whether my brief interaction with Herr Klaus might illuminate other social spaces in the society he lived in and show how his inn fit into a greater whole, namely German culture—or at an even higher level, into global culture. To create such a complex and inclusive picture would require picking up particular cultural strands— objects, actions, figures of speech and discourse—that run across distinct social domains and weaving them together to represent that greater whole, showing the continuities as well as the rips and tears within it.

One such connecting thread that an anthropologist can use to stitch together a larger picture is an account of his or her own personal and social development. In this German context, this account might be aptly called the anthropologist's *Bildung*. The distinctively German concept of *Bildung*, or "self-formation…can be defined as individual education, understood as intellectual, moral, and spiritual fulfilment, derived from the Enlightenment promise of self-realization, yet inalterably linked with the Pietist concepts of introspection and duty in the community" (Myers 2004: 15) [*sic*]. Reflecting the strong influence of German thought on the early development of anthropology, the *Bildung* ideal helped shape the discipline as a self-reflexive social science that unites "cultural understanding with personal development" (Peacock 2002: 50). Although preeminently a nineteenth-century ideal, the notion of *Bildung* left a lasting imprint on both anthropology and German culture. It is perhaps unsurprising, then, that my reflections on my stay with Herr Klaus share some features with the traditional *Bildungsroman*, or novel of self-formation, which shows "how the initially callow but open-minded and lively hero had after varied experiences and innumerable discussions with people of all kinds found his feet in the world" (Bruford 1975: 224).

A *Bildungsroman* tends to end "happily and with the implication that with the lessons he had learnt, the hero was ready for whatever the future might bring" (224).[19] While anthropological accounts often document tragedy and do not end on a happy note, the anthropologists themselves can be likened to heroes in a *Bildungsroman*; they emerge from their research accounts as wise and well prepared to engage in further research. Insofar that I can draw on the idea of the *Bildungsroman* to illuminate the way that I come across in this book, then my representation of the inn and host–guest interaction fit into a greater whole that is, in part, an aspect of German culture, and, at a higher level, through cultural anthropology, an aspect of global culture.

I will conclude the first chapter of this book, then, with a description of my departure from Herr Klaus's apartment. For in the end, my experiences inside the inn did serve as a sort of preparation for what I would occasionally encounter outside it, in the former East Germany: frustration and sadness, fantasies and threats of violence, and a code of honor drawn from a subtext of heterosexual masculinity.

LEAVING THE SAFE SPACE OF THE INN

I came back at four in the afternoon. Herr Klaus met me in the hallway. "You're back. When are you going to vacate the room?"

I told Herr Klaus that I would be gone by five, and went to my room. The sheets had been stripped from my bed, exposing a thick blue mattress. The duvet blanket had been folded in half.

Braving the cold, I spent my last hour at the inn writing postcards to friends and family in the States. At five I knocked on the living room door, and Herr Klaus came out. I noticed a pillow and a blanket on the living room sofa. He had taken a nap, apparently. But he was not alone: standing behind him was a short, stocky man who promptly introduced himself, with a shy smile, as Herr Klaus's son. He insisted on helping me with my heavier suitcase. "I can do it. I work as a cab driver. I live upstairs."

I was glad that he was nicer than his father. Was he compensating for his father's grumpiness?

It was dark, cold, and drizzling outside as I wheeled my suitcases to the tram stop at the edge of the small square. A week and a half ago, when I first arrived, I had walked here in the evening and had been struck by the square's beauty. That night, like today, it was already dark and there was a light rain falling. Except for a man walking a big black dog and the anthropologist on his first day of fieldwork, the square was just as deserted and still then as it was now. The deciduous trees once again glowed a burnt yellow in the soft light of the street lamps; the church, blackened by coal smoke, remained imposing and grand.

A middle-aged couple was standing at the tram stop. After we had waited together in silence for fifteen minutes, they walked off. Shortly thereafter, I saw a young couple approaching. I turned away to glance at the tram schedule.

From close behind me, I heard the man say, "The tram won't come."

I turned around to face him; rather than step back to give me space, he came even closer. He stared at me. When I finally took a step back, he grunted. He was a menacing young man.

"Leave him alone," the woman said.

"Shit," he said, continuing to stare at me. I was starting to feel very uncomfortable.

She called out to him again: "Come over here!"

Finally, he left. I decided to walk over to the Intercontinental Hotel and grab a cab.

NOTES

1. The confusion between host and guest emerges as an important theme in the second part of this book, where I discuss Airbnb and the potential that extreme hostility, or horror, would put an end to hospitality.

2. I do not have evidence of Herr Klaus expressing loyalty to local authorities as a means to please or reward his guests. This point exposes one weakness of my argument in this chapter: my reliance on a single case.

3. "Transaction gives recognition to the possibility of the host–guest relations involving nonreciprocal relations" (McIntosh et al. 2011: 511).

4. There are multiple editions of Freyer's book. The link in the bibliography to the website that features Freyer's work would likely feature the latest edition, rather than the 2006 edition to which I refer to here.

5. Walter Freyer does not indicate the exact years to which the 80-percent figure applies.

6. My book can be framed as a contribution to the literature on how East Germans coped with the aftermath of the reunification and, more generally, how people in the former Eastern Bloc adapted to the fall of the Iron Curtain. Two other contributors to this extensive literature, Nora Dudwick and Hermine De Soto, made the following very interesting statement: "In contrast with the stability or 'stagnancy' of socialism, citizens of post-socialist countries now find themselves confronting a rapidly mutating 'past' and an unpredictable future. They understand that they are going

through some kind of transition—although even this has become a contested concept—but they have no clear sense of where they are headed. They feel shock and indignation at the sudden and extreme decline in their economic and symbolic status" (Dudwick and De Soto 2000: 4). Although they were speaking of post-socialist Europe as a whole, Dudwick and De Soto captured the predicament of many people I encountered in eastern Germany.

7. Kanafani-Zahar 1983: 100.

8. It is tempting to speculate that the two recurring phrases that Herr Klaus used to reprimand me—"this is your problem" and "you must decide"—could be traced back to a particular time in his life. Were these phrases used in conversations in the recent past with lawyers and other officials concerning the status of his apartment? Did they hark back to exchanges that he had with East German state security officials interested in containing the threat posed by his foreign guests? It is conceivable, too, that the words could be traced back to experiences he had during World War II and its aftermath, times of trauma and dislocation for so many in his generation.

9. Anthropologists recognize that, heuristically, punishments have varied aims and audiences. A punishment might be exacted to repair one's public reputation; the audience for such retaliation is made up of the individuals with whom one negotiates changes in one's social standing. Or a punishment might be carried out to repair one's self-image; here, the principal audience is oneself. I believe that Herr Klaus's punishments were carried out principally for his own gratification, as he sought to repair his self-image by denigrating an individual who failed to value the favor he offered. However, it is also possible that he related the stories of his skirmishes and victories during my stay to his son, his daughter, other relatives, or friends.

10. In the former East Germany, these basic data—and, at times, additional insights about the guests—were valued by the Stasi.

11. I do not have evidence of Herr Klaus expressing the value of loyalty to local authorities as a means of drawing closer to his guests. While I can imagine scenarios in which an innkeeper might do so, it is possible that, as a general rule, innkeepers express allegiance to local authorities in situations when they are seeking to create distance between themselves and their guests.

12. There are numerous institutional forms of hospitality in Germany that fall outside the purview of this study: unpaid hospitality rendered to family members and friends, hospitality in church settings, hospitality offered to local and foreign dignitaries, etc. I would expect the values of hospitality to vary somewhat across these forms. For example, the value of economizing seems to be absent from the hospitality that was

extended to dignitaries. In the early middle ages, government representatives enjoyed a right to hospitality that was specific to them and was called the *Gastungsrecht der Obrigkeit*, or the authorities' right to hospitality. It allowed officials to demand free accommodations for the night (Jenn 1993: 13). The *Gastungsrecht* also "recalls the feudal right of medieval lords in German-speaking lands and neighboring regions in western and central Europe to be housed (and fed) indefinitely at the manors of any of their vassals" (Miles Becker, personal correspondence, October 2013).

13. It is important to note here that some pubs also served as inns; as mentioned earlier, the German word for innkeeper, Wirt, also means pub owner.

14. Reflecting on the shift away from the *hujera*, Lindholm notes, "At the time of my fieldwork [1977], cooperation in the neighbourhood had greatly diminished following the decrease in the importance of the hujera and the power of the khan over his clients" (1982: 229). Rather than wish to donate food to the guests who were hosted at the *hujera*, people increasingly preferred to sell their surplus foodstuffs "... to get money for the purchase of status item" (229).

15. A decline in hospitality can be contextualized as just one aspect of a more general decline in ritual participation, such as has been observed by some anthropologists in parts of eastern Europe (Creed 2002: 70). Sometime in the future, when circumstances change again, one might expect hospitality to be revived with a great deal of nostalgia.

16. Ian Campbell argues that the persistence of generosity in Polynesian hospitality is due to the fact that Polynesians did not follow a rigid set of practices, but acted pragmatically (1981: 35). While his argument bears some similarity to my argument about resilient practices of hospitality accommodating hostility, our arguments differ with respect to a crucial point: Campbell describes a set of encounters between visitors and locals. In some encounters the locals recognize the strangers as guests and offer hospitality. In other encounters they do not extend hospitality and engage in hostile actions instead. In contrast, I argue that hostility is weaved into the very practice of hospitality. In the second part of this book, where I explore how extreme hostility puts an end to hospitality, I do so with reference to the concept of horror.

17. Andrew Shryock notes that hospitality lends itself to analogies that involve a shift of scale from household, to ethnic group, to the state (2012: S20). Examining *karam* or hospitality, in Jordan, he notes that "this movement from *karam* to 'universal hospitality', then back again, is enabled by the scalar elasticity of hospitality itself, which is always of a place but inherently transportable. Designed for travel and to receive the traveller, hospitality is a motif open to extension and endless analogy" (S23).

18. Each of these dyads implies a unique power dynamic. In the second part of this book, I examine further the power differences between hosts and guests, noting that in the context of Airbnb, hosts and guests are sometimes called "peers"—they are part of the peer-to-peer economy—a label that suggests parity.

19. There are exceptions to this pattern. Some famous examples of the Bildungsroman do not have happy endings. Thomas Mann's *The Magic Mountain*, for example, "can be said 'almost to parody' this kind of novel in that the hero comes to terms, in the course of it, not so much with life as with death, or at least with death as the ever-present shadow of life" (Bruford 1975: 224). Taking account of the many and varied appropriations and reinterpretations of the Bildung ideal in the twentieth century is beyond the scope of this work. It is worth briefly noting, however, the interpretation of Günter de Bruyn's 1984 novel *Neue Herrlichkeit* that has been proposed by Valerie Greenberg. In Greenberg's view, de Bruyn draws on Mann's novel and the Bildung ideal to criticize East German society. In *Neue Herrlichkeit*, there is no "epiphany" or "affirmation of selfhood of the wholeness and significance of the subject who goes on, bettered by a transformative experience" (1987: 208). Such an epiphany would have implied "development, continuity with history, the worth of learning, the existence and value of the personality with its capacity for growth and change" (208). De Bruyn's novel, according to Greenberg, implies that East German society did not provide the necessary conditions for such a process of self-formation.

References

Arpaci, Annette Seidel. 2008. Better Germans? 'Hostipitality' and Strategic Creolization in Maxim Biller's Writings. *Thamyris/Intersecting* 19: 159–180.

Bahr, Hans-Dieter. 1994. *Die Sprache des Gastes: Eine Metaethik*. Leipzig: Reclam Verlag.

Barth, Fredrik. 1981. Pathan Identity and its Maintenance. In *Features of Person and Society in Swat: Collected Essays on Pathans. Selected Essays of Fredrik Barth*, Vol. II, 103–120. London: Routledge and Kegan Paul.

Benhabib, Seyla. 2005. On the Alleged Conflict between Democracy and International Law. *Ethics & International Affairs* 19(1): 85–100.

Bruford, Walter Horace. 1975. *The German Tradition of Self-Cultivation: 'Bildung' from Humbolt to Thomas Mann*. Cambridge: Cambridge University Press.

Campbell, Ian. 1981. Of Polynesian Hospitality. *Journal De La Société Des Océanistes* 37(70–71): 27–37.

Chambers, Erve. 2000. *Native Tours: The Anthropology of Travel and Tourism*. Prospect Heights, Ill: Waveland Press.

Coles, Tim. 2003. Urban tourism, place promotion and economic restructuring: The case of post-socialist Leipzig. *Tourism Geographies* 5(2): 190–219.

Colson, Elizabeth. 1989. Overview. *Annual Review of Anthropology* 18: 1–17.

Creed, Gerald W. 2002. Economic Crisis and Ritual Decline in Eastern Europe. In *Postsocialism: Ideals, Ideologies, and Practices in Eurasia*, ed. C.M. Hann, 57–73. London: Routledge.

Crick, Malcolm. 1989. Representations of International Tourism in the Social Sciences: Sun, Sex, Sights, Savings, and Servility. *Annual Review of Anthropology* 18: 307–344.

De Soto, Hermine. 2000. Crossing Western Boundaries: How East Berlin Women Observed Women Researchers from the West after Socialism, 1991–1992. In *Fieldwork Dilemmas: Anthropologists in Postsocialist States*, eds. Hermine De Soto and Nora Dudwick, 73–99. Madison: The University of Wisconsin Press.

Deutsches Wörterbuch, ed. 2000. Renate Wahrig-Burfeind. Munich: Bertelsmann Lexikon Verlag.

Derrida, Jacques, and Anne Dufourmantelle. 2000. *Of hospitality*. Stanford, CA: Stanford University Press.

Di Domenico, MariaLaura, and Peter Fleming. 2009. 'It's a Guesthouse Not a Brothel': Policing Sex in the Home-Workplace. *Human Relations* 62(2): 245–269.

Dikeç, Mustafa, Nigel Clark, and Clive Barnett. 2009. Extending Hospitality: Giving Space, Taking Time. *Paragraph: A Journal of Modern Critical Theory* 32(1): 1–14.

Dudwick, Nora, and Hermine De Soto. 2000. Introduction. In *Fieldwork Dilemmas: Anthropologists in Postsocialist States*, eds. Hermine De Soto and Nora Dudwick, 195–217. Madison: The University of Wisconsin Press.

Freyer, Walter. 2006. *Tourismus: Einführung in die Fremdenverkehrsökonomie*. Munich:Oldenbourg Wissenschaftsverlag. http://books.google.com/books?id=SavFTEuUG9oC&printsec=frontcover#v=onepage&q=interflug&f=false. Accessed November 9, 2014.

Friedrich-Ebert-Stiftung. 1985. *Urlaub und Tourismus in beiden deutschen Staaten*. Bonn: Verlag Neue Gesellschaft.

Friese, Heidrun. 2003. Der Gast: Zum Verhältnis von Ethnologie und Philosophie. *Deutsche Zeitschrift Für Philosophie* 51(2): 311–324. http://www.hfriese.de/download_files/der%20gast%20zfph.pdf. Accessed November 9, 2014.

Friese, Heidrun. 2010. The Limits of Hospitality: Political Philosophy. *Undocumented Migration and the Local Arena. European Journal of Social Theory* 13(3): 323–341.

Görlich, Christopher. 2006–2007. Urlaub vom Staat. Zur Geschichte des Tourismus in der DDR. *Potsdamer Bulletin für Zeithistorische Studien*. 36-37/2006 and Nr. 38-39/2007: 64–68. http://www.zzf-pdm.de/Portals/_Rainbow/images/publikationen/Goerlich_38.pdf. Accessed May 14, 2012.

Greenberg, Valerie D. 1987. Günter de Bruyn's Neue Herrlichkeit: Leveling the Zauberberg. *The German Quarterly* 60(2): 205–219.

Hachtmann, Rüdiger. 2007. *Tourismus-Geschichte*. Göttingen: Vandenhoeck & Ruprecht.

Hamington, Maurice. 2010. *Feminism and Hospitality: Gender in the Host/Guest Relationship*. Lanham: Lexington Books.

Herzfeld, Michael. 1987. 'As In Your Own House': Hospitality, Ethnography, and the Stereotype of Mediterranean Society. In *Honor and Shame and the Unity of the Mediterranean*, ed. David D. Gilmore, 75–89. Washington: American Anthropological Association.

Herzfeld, Michael. 2000. Afterword: Intimations from an Uncertain Place. In *Fieldwork Dilemmas: Anthropologists in Postsocialist States*, eds. Hermine G. De Soto and Nora Dudwick, 219–235. Madison: The University of Wisconsin Press.

Hite, Katherine. 2015. Empathic Unsettlement and the Outsider within Argentine Spaces of Memory. *Memory Studies* 8 (1): 38–48. Published online before print on October 8, 2014. http://mss.sagepub.com/content/early/2014/10/07/1750698014552407. Accessed November 5, 2014.

Jenn, Albrecht. 1993. *Die deutsche Gastronomie: Eine historische und betriebswirtschaftliche Betrachtung*. Frankfurt am Main: Deutscher Fachverlag.

Kanafani-Zahar, Aïda. 1983. *Aesthetics and Ritual in the United Arab Emirates: The Anthropology of Food and Personal Adornment Among Arabian Women*. Beirut: American University of Beirut.

Kanafani-Zahar, Aïda. 2002. *Kluge: Etymologisches Wörterbuch der deutschen Sprache*, 24th ed. Edited by Elmar Seebold. Berlin: Walter de Gruyter.

Kenna, Margaret E. 2010. Foreword. In *Thinking through Tourism*, eds. Julie Scott and Tom Selwyn, xiii–xxiv. Oxford: Berg.

Koda, Yoshiki. 2009. Synthese von Nähe und Ferne. Kulturhistorische überlegungen zu drei Modellen der Gastfreundschaft im europäischen Mittelalter. In Figuren des Transgressiven: das Ende und der Gast, ed. Kanichiro Omiya, 235–251. München: Iudicium.

Kolinsky, Eva. 1998. In Search of a Future: Leipzig Since the Wende. *German Politics & Society* 16(4): 103–121.

Kuehnast, Kathleen. 2000. Ethnographic Encounters in Post-Soviet Kyrgyzstan: Dilemmas of Gender, Poverty, and the Cold War. In *Fieldwork Dilemmas: Anthropologists in Postsocialist States*, eds. Hermine G. De Soto and Nora Dudwick, 100–118. Madison: The University of Wisconsin Press.

Ladner, Sam. 2014. *Practical Ethnography: A Guide to Doing Ethnography in the Private Sector*. Walnut Park, CA: Left Coast Press, Inc.

Lenz, Ramona. 2010. 'Hotel Royal' and other Spaces of Hospitality: Tourists and Migration in the Mediterranean. In *Thinking through Tourism*, eds. Julie Scott and Tom Selwyn, 209–229. Oxford: Berg.

Lindholm, Charles. 1982. *Generosity and Jealousy: Swat Pukhtun of Northern Pakistan*. New York: Columbia University Press.

McNulty, Tracy. 2007. *The Hostess: Hospitality, Femininity, and the Expropriation of Identity*. Minneapolis: University of Minnesota Press.

McIntosh, Alison J., Paul Lynch, and Majella Sweeney. 2011. 'My Home Is My Castle': Defiance of the Commercial Homestay Host in Tourism. *Journal of Travel Research* 50(5): 509–519.

Mellor, E.H. 1991. Eastern Germany (the former German Democratic Republic). In *Tourism and Economic Development in Eastern Europe and the Soviet Union*, ed. Derek R. Hall, 142–153. London: Belhaven Press.

Melville, Peter. 2007. *Romantic Hospitality and the Resistance to Accommodation*. Waterloo: Wilfrid Laurier University Press.

Molz, Jennie Germann, and Sarah Gibson. 2007. *Mobilizing Hospitality: The Ethics of Social Relations in a Mobile World*. Aldershot: Ashgate.

Myers, Perry. 2004. *The Double-Edged Sword: The Cult of Bildung, its Downfall and Reconstitution in Fin-de-Siècle Germany*. German Linguistic and Cultural Studies, 11. Bern: Peter Lang.

Myers, Perry. 2005. *Oxford-Duden German Dictionary: German-English, English-German*, eds. Michael Clark and Olaf Thyen, 3rd ed. Oxford: Oxford University Press.

Peacock, James. 2002. Action Comparison: Efforts Towards a Global and Comparative yet Local and Active Anthropology. In *Anthropology, by Comparison*, eds. Andre Gingrich and Richard G. Fox, 44–69. London: Routledge.

Pechlaner, Harald, and Frieda Raich. 2007. Wettbewerbsfähigkeit durch das Zusammenspiel von Gastlichkeit und Gastfreundschaft. In *Gastfreundschaft und Gastlichkeit im Tourismus: Kundenzufriedenheit und –bindung mit Hospitality Management*, eds. Harald Pechlaner and Frieda Raich, 11–24. Berlin: Erich Schmidt Verlag.

Polese, Abel. 2009. The Guest at the Dining Table: Economic Transitions and the Reshaping of Hospitality—Reflections from Batumi and Odessa. *Anthropology of East Europe Review* 27(1): 76–87.

Schimmelpfennig, Roland. 2011. *The Golden Dragon [Der Goldene Drache]*. Washington, D.C: Studio Theater. November 3.

Schrutka-Rechtenstamm, Adelheid. 1997a. Gäste and Gastgeber: Touristische Ritualisierungen diesseits und jenseits der Bezahlung. *Tourismus Journal* 1(3/4): 467–481.

Schrutka-Rechtenstamm, Adelheid. 1997b. Vom Mythos Gastfreundschaft. In *"Herzlich Willkommen!" Rituale der Gastlichkeit*, ed. Ulrike Kammerhofer-Aggermann, 47–56. Salzburg: Salzburger Landesinstitut für Volkskunde.

Seebold, Elmar, ed. 2002. Kluge: Etymologisches Wörterbuch der deutschen Sprache. 24th ed. Berlin: Walter de Gruyter.

Sherman, Rachel. 2005. Producing the Superior Self: Strategic Comparison and Symbolic Boundaries among Luxury Hotel Workers. *Ethnography* 6(2): 131–158.

Shryock, Andrew. 2004. The New Jordanian Hospitality: House, Host, and Guest in the Culture of Public Display. *Comparative Studies in Society and History* 46(1): 35–62.

Shryock, Andrew. 2012. Breaking Hospitality Apart: Bad Hosts, Bad Guests, and the Problem of Sovereignty. *Journal of the Royal Anthropological Institute* 18: S20–S33.

Touval, Amitai. 2005. The Coping Strategy of Women Members of the Former East German Intelligentsia. *Journal for the Society of the Anthropology of Europe* 5(2): 13–20.

Touval, Amitai. 2011. The Pastoral, Nostalgia, and Political Power in Leipzig, Germany. *Urbanities* 1(1): 43–53.

Touval, Amitai. 2013. Local Knowledge of Elites as a Basis for Comparing Political Systems. *Anthropology of East Europe Review* 31(2): 46–62.

Touval, Amitai. 2014. Peripheral Observations as a Source of Innovation. *Urbanities.* 4(2): 100–103.

Von Kardorff, Ursula. 1958. *Feste feiern wie sie fallen: Gastlichkeit früher und Heute.* Munich: Biederstein Verlag.

Wallner, Ernst Maxim. 1968. *Von der Herberge zum Grandhotel; Wirtshäuser und Gastlichkeit: Geschichte, Wirtshausnamen, Wirtshausschilder.* Konstanz: Rosgarten Verlag.

Wernhart, Karl R. 1997. Rituale der Gastlichkeit. Kulturanthropologische Universalien. In *"Herzlich Willkommen!" Rituale der Gastlichkeit*, ed. Ulrike Kammerhofer–Aggermann, 23–33. Salzburg: Salzburger Landesinstitut für Volkskunde.

Wood, Roy C. 1994a. Hotel Culture and Social Control. *Annals of Tourism Research* 21: 65–80.

Wood, Roy C. 1994b. Some Theoretical Perspective on Hospitality. In *Tourism: The State of the Art*, ed. A.V. Seaton, 737–742. Chichester: Wiley.

CHAPTER 2

Airbnb

Abstract I returned to Leipzig in the summer of 2015 and stayed at an Airbnb. Leipzig has overcome a recent history of decline, and consisted with this development, my Airbnb hostess was fond of travel.

I argue that Airbnb hosts and guests resemble each other, a mirroring that alters the power dynamics between them.

The value of advising the guests has been reimagined in response to the digital revolution, and the value of allegiance to local authorities has been greatly diminished. Interestingly, there was no place for the expression hostility, except online through Airbnb's rating mechanism.

I conclude by considering what Airbnb horror stories, or failed hospitality, can tell us about Airbnb's unique contribution to hospitality.

Keywords Airbnb · Hospitality · Rating mechanism · Allegiance to local authorities · Failed hospitality · Horror

HOSPITALITY IN THE DIGITAL AGE

In June 2015, I took a Singapore Airlines flight from New York City to Frankfurt. Upon my arrival in Germany, I boarded the first intercity express ICE train to Leipzig. I was eager to return to Leipzig for another extended stay. The purpose of this trip to Leipzig was not to investigate hospitality, but rather to revisit the Rosa Luxemburg Foundation and learn about the persistence of the East German intelligentsia after

© The Author(s) 2017   41
A. Touval, *An Anthropological Study of Hospitality*,
DOI 10.1007/978-3-319-42049-3_2

reunification. After returning home to New York several weeks later, however, I realized that the Internet had transformed the experience of hospitality in a manner that I could not have predicted, casting hospitality in a new light.

The first part of this manuscript refers to events that took place in 1996. At that time, accessing the web meant dialing a local number that belonged to an Internet provider (such as AOL) and patiently waiting to connect as the computer emitted syncopated, insect-like chirps. By 2015, this soundtrack had vanished, its closest descendent being the whale-like sounds of Skype.

Likewise, the digital age has seen the emergence of a robust ecosystem of new forms of hospitality, including global online platforms such as Airbnb that propagate hosts and guests in neighborhoods and buildings in which they might clash with neighbors and housing advocates.[1] The spatially nested concepts of household, city, and country remain valid for contextualizing the interaction between hosts and guests, as valid at an Airbnb in 2015 as they were at Herr Klaus's inn in 1996. At the same time, Airbnb facilitates the virtual flow of ideas, media, and money, making it necessary for both participants and observers to create a narrative that is less bound by time and place.[2]

Thus, in this second part of my book, I analyze my interaction with an Airbnb hostess by exploring our virtual interaction on Airbnb's online platform and our face-to-face interaction over the six days I spent as a guest in her apartment. To provide a broader account of both my Airbnb hostess and Airbnb itself, I also describe Leipzig and its hospitality industry in 2015. I revisit the values of economizing, advising the guest, and allegiance to local authorities that I identified during my stay with Herr Klaus in 1996, and I uncover new themes, such as the host as consummate traveler and the relative parity between Airbnb hosts and their guests. In the anthropology of hospitality, hosts dominate the immediate circumstances in which hospitality takes place, but when one enlarges the frame of reference, guests have more power than their hosts do. Somewhat similarly, Airbnb guests are in a more secure position than Airbnb hosts, because of the controversies surrounding Airbnb. Airbnb is reputed to disrupt local rental markets when some of the hosts in its network violate laws designed to protect renters. This negative reputation can put hosts on the defensive. Moreover, Airbnb takes an active role in shaping the power dynamic between hosts and guests through its rating mechanism, with the potential of a hostile review further tipping the balance of power in favor of guests. The rating mechanism is also a management technique for enforcing accountability, as hosts or guests who are described as failing to perform their proper roles can be removed from Airbnb's network.

In popular media, accounts of deeply disappointing Airbnb experiences are often referred to as "Airbnb horror stories." Reading through the anthropological literature, I propose a framework for organizing incidents of what I call "failed hospitality." Failed hospitality is conceptually distinct from the theme of hostility that I explored in the first part of this book in connection with the innkeeper, Herr Klaus. I conclude by suggesting new directions for further research on these topics.

Hospitality in a Changed City

Arriving in Leipzig by train on the afternoon of June 11, I had a few hours to explore the city before my appointment with the Airbnb hostess. An innkeeper would likely have let me in earlier. Folded into the role of innkeeper is the task of waiting in a fixed location, the inn, for peripatetic (and often adventurous) guests. This was not required of my Airbnb hostess. She was a working professional, and my arrival time had been specifically set for eight o'clock in the evening.

I began by exploring the city's main train station. Though I had visited Leipzig in the intervening years, this time the contrast to 1996 seemed particularly stark. Back then, the rich smell of wood treated with creosote hung along the platform, and the walls of the station's majestic main hall had been blackened by coal smoke. In 2015, I detected only a faint whiff of creosote at the end of the platform. While the train announcements were still preceded by a three-note ringtone in a descending scale, the kits of pigeons that had once orchestrated a lively backdrop were gone. The spacious interior had been cleaned and transformed into a shopping mall.

I had soup at one of the terminal's Asian restaurants, purchased a SIM card in the basement, and then exited the station and crossed the wide ring road to a new transit information center. I showed the attendant my small collection of tram tickets from my previous visits in 2000 and 2007. Since my old tickets could not be exchanged for a new card, I offered them to him for his private collection, and he happily accepted.

Buoyed by this brief encounter, I floated through the city's old medieval core, which now looked pristine and wealthy. I passed large shopping malls teeming with shoppers. New office towers had displaced socialist-era apartment buildings. In what had been one of the big empty spaces downtown—the legacy of Allied bombing raids during World War II—was now a giant glass box, the city's new Museum of Fine Arts.

Back in 1996, Leipzig was in demographic decline, and despite the massive effort the city was making to renovate its housing stock and infrastructure, it was difficult to foresee a resurgence. In 1995, the annual number of births in Leipzig hit a low of 2377, down from 6792 in 1986.[3] On the first morning of my 1996 stay, Herr Klaus had complained that the playground across the street would soon be replaced by a building that would block his view of downtown. A few months later, I attended meetings at city hall in which citizens protested against closings of kindergartens and schools. The city's decline was so precipitous that by 2000 Leipzig and other cities in eastern Germany were at the center of a public debate about the future of "shrinking cities" (in German, *schrumpfende Städte*) (Florentin 2010: 87). Leipzig's response to the growing "patches of waste land" that "perforated" the urban landscape (87) was hampered by ballooning public debt, which by 2000 had reached 860 million euros (94).

Yet despite these difficulties, Leipzig ultimately succeeded in reversing course and attracting businesses and people. The city's population started to grow again, rising from 493,208 in 2000 to 544,479 in 2014,[4] and consistent with this demographic change, the annual number of births has steadily climbed and is now close to its 1980s levels.[5] In 1996, during my stay with Herr Klaus, the unemployment rate was around 18 percent (Garcia-Zamor 2008: 144), while in 2015 it was below 10 percent—still high but nevertheless a tremendous improvement.[6] Another indicator of the city's growing attractiveness is tourism. By 2013, tourism was bringing one-and-a-half billion euros to Leipzig per year (Neumann et al. n.d.: 15). In 2013, hotels had an 85-percent share of visitors' expenditures on overnight accommodations in Leipzig (6); there were 117 hotels in the city, with an occupancy rate of 50.7 percent (29).

Airbnb has a small but growing presence in the market for overnight accommodations in Leipzig. With its 790 Airbnbs, Leipzig ranks seventh on the list of German cities with the most Airbnb listings. The city just below it on the list, Nürnberg, has far fewer listings, only 484. The next city down the list, Dresden, has 447.[7] The relatively high number of Airbnb listings in Leipzig might be the outcome of several interrelated factors.[8] First, Leipzig has a long history of encouraging its residents, both individuals and families, to host out-of-town visitors who are attending the city's trade shows each spring and fall (Kolinsky 1998: 104). Airbnb hosts could be seen as part of this long tradition of hospitality. Second, Leipzig has weathered a period of decline during which there was a strong desire in the city to see more of its housing stock renovated and reoccupied (Florentin 2010). Airbnb can be perceived as contributing to increased demand in the city's housing market. Leipzig has also had persistently high rates of unemployment, another legacy of its period of decline. Airbnb is a source of revenue for city residents, for hosts as well shopkeepers and other service providers who sell products and services to Airbnb guests while they are staying in Leipzig. The city recognizes the importance of tourist dollars. A report published on the city's website states that in 2013 visitors to Leipzig spent more than 1.3 billion euros on shopping, food, and entertainment (Neumann et al. n.d.: 19). Third, Leipzig has a tradition of being welcoming to strangers, a commitment which has been recently put to the test by movements such as PEGIDA and LEGIDA that have staged demonstrations in Leipzig and elsewhere in Germany against the country's liberal immigration policy, especially as it applies to Muslims, and against the presence of asylum-seekers in residential neighborhoods. Many Leipzig residents—including the mayor, Burkhard Jung—have participated in demonstrations against PEGIDA and LEGIDA, calling for the protection of the rights of asylum-seekers regardless of their religious persuasion and speaking out in favor of integrating asylum seekers into the larger society. I expect that for many people in Leipzig, the presence of asylum-seekers is much more strongly felt than the presence of Airbnbs, and the conflict over immigration overshadows any controversies that might arise over Airbnb. Furthermore, I expect the arguments of the pro-asylum-seekers' coalition to be consistent with tolerating Airbnb.

Yet elsewhere in Germany, housing advocates and local governments are resisting Airbnb. Airbnb has been the subject of criticism and regulatory action in Berlin, Frankfurt, and other German cities (Hill 2015; Kotowsky 2014a; Kotowsky 2014b). One possible direction for future research would be to investigate how local stakeholders in Leipzig discuss Airbnb, including how they react to news about the conflicts that Airbnb has sparked in other cities.

A Diminished Allegiance to Local Authorities

In 1996, the capsule descriptions in my travel guide were minimal but sufficient. Only a few inns were listed. I did not know in advance what my room at Herr Klaus's would look like, but I knew his address and phone number. The addresses of inns were public information, published in guidebooks and available at the local tourist office.

For his part, the innkeeper did not know much about me, which explains why his initial stance was so guarded. To vet prospective guests over the phone, the innkeeper would ask only a few basic questions: where are you coming from, whom are you coming with, and what is the purpose of your visit? The vulnerability of innkeepers was what made it necessary for them to be allied with local authorities.

Airbnb hosts are less exposed than innkeepers, for two main reasons. First, Airbnb hosts do not disclose their exact address to prospective guests. Guests receive their host's address only after their host has approved their application and they have paid for their stay. Second, Airbnb offers hosts and guests a powerful tool, an online profile with comments from previous hosts and guests, for establishing their mutual credentials and thus minimizing the danger that each potentially poses to the other.

Searching for accommodations on Airbnb prior to my arrival in Leipzig, I identified a dozen profiles that included a description of the amenities and photos of the hosts, the rooms they had on offer, and previous guests' comments about their hosts. Guests might compliment their hosts for the breakfasts they were served; for the cleanliness and comforts of the bedroom in which they stayed; for small touches, such as being offered toiletries; or for making the arrangements as uncomplicated as possible. This background information created a sense of familiarity and reduced the perceived risk of a surprise, whether positive or negative.

As a potential guest, I too had a profile on Airbnb, with feedback in English from two previous hosts that served to establish my credentials. Potential hosts in Leipzig could use Google Translate to read my profile in German; potentially more reassuring still, they could learn even more about me by searching my name on Google.

After identifying a potential hostess by the name of Gretchen (a pseudonym), I contacted her through the Airbnb messaging system. Her profile indicated that guests who planned to stay more than a few days had some kitchen privileges. I applied to stay at her home for six days before moving into a studio apartment, and wrote (in English) to ask whether I could store food in the fridge. I included in my message information that I hoped would further qualify me as a guest. "My purpose in Leipzig is research (anthropology)," I wrote, "I lived on Klasing Street back in 1996–1997." I entered my payment information, a crucial step in completing my credentials on Airbnb. This was an option that Herr Klaus did not have in 1996. The lack of a payment guarantee was another point of vulnerability that expedited the innkeeper's allegiance to local authorities.

Gretchen responded briefly in German, accepting me as a guest and saying that there would be a shelf in the fridge for me to use. "Hallo Amitai, JA—Du kannst gern bei mir wohnen. Im Kühlschrank gibt es ein Fach für Dich:-) Herzichen Gruß von [Gretchen]." I thanked her. I now had a place to stay in Leipzig.

I heard back from Gretchen two weeks later:

> Hallo Amitai, ich bin jetzt bis zum 9.6. in Spanien auf dm Jakobsweg. Am 10.06. bin ich wieder zu Hause, falls Du noch einmal Kontakt aufnehmen möchtest. Einchecken am 11. 6. gegen 10 Uhr oder ab ca. 20 Uhr. Bis dahin, herzlichen Gruß von [Gretchen]

She reported that she would be in Spain until June 9, traveling the pilgrimage route of Santiago de Compostela, and that if I would like to contact her, she would be back home on June 10. She requested that I check in by ten in the morning or after eight in the evening.

This brief interaction already revealed that my hostess was playing the role of the worldly traveler—letting it be known that she too enjoyed going abroad, while assuring her guest that she would be back in her hometown just in time to host him. The calendar feature on Airbnb's website allowed her to pace herself, marking the days on which she would like to make the room available, and to fix the price of the accommodations as she saw fit, in competition with the prices set by other Leipzig hosts.

THE HOME AS AN INN

It was a couple of minutes after eight when I arrived at the Airbnb address, a well-maintained apartment building that seemed to be about twenty years old. I was buzzed in and took the elevator up. On Gretchen's profile, I could see that she was older than I, perhaps in her mid-50s, but also that she preferred to be on a first name-basis with her guests. I had also noted that in our brief correspondence, she had used the informal variant of the German second-person pronoun. With Herr Klaus I was never on such familiar terms, and when he employed the informal second person, his purpose was to put me in my place.

Since I had seen her photo on Airbnb, I immediately recognized Gretchen when she opened the door to greet me. We were standing in a long corridor decorated with a wood-framed mirror, a vase with dried flowers, and modern paintings. She asked me about my trip and then showed me around the apartment. The first door to the left was the toilet, and the second was the bathroom. She opened the door across from the bathroom, and I instantly recognized the bedroom from the photos that she had posted on her Airbnb profile, except that it was larger than I had expected.

Although her profile did not specify that breakfast was included, Gretchen inquired what I would like for breakfast the next day. Did I want bread, cereal, fruit, and yogurt? It was a gesture of generosity that I did not expect. Hoping to make a stronger connection with her, I mentioned that the purpose of my visit to Leipzig was to do research at the Rosa Luxemburg Foundation, and she reciprocated by saying that she liked Rosa Luxemburg, signaling that her politics were left of center. I then asked about her trip to Spain, but to this question she responded in a cursory, non-descriptive manner. Recognizing that she had just got back from her journey the day before and was likely still tired, I was careful not to pursue the subject and risk imposing on her privacy. I knew that we would be asked to rate each other on the Airbnb website next week, so I checked my curiosity.

I settled into my bedroom, tired but happy to see sunny, light-blue skies outside the windows, even though it was past eight in the evening. A local landmark peeked above the rooftops of the apartment houses across the street, making the room seem that much more special. The two windows had, on the inside, wide sills that supported four potted plants. The walls were decorated with original art: three paintings of flowers, a poster with image of an Indian goddess, and another artwork from India.[9] On the old desk was a bowl filled with individually wrapped Italian chocolates, and to the right of the desk, leaning against the wall, was a guitar.

As I unpacked my suitcase that night, I noticed that at the foot of the bed there was a basket of toiletries: shampoo, razor, soaps, shaving cream, and a small towel. She may have collected these amenities on her travels, an implication which accentuated her image as someone who has traveled the world—herself an occasional guest, who, when at home, plays host. At many inns, the proprietors—sometimes successfully, sometimes less so—attempt to make their rooms feel like a bedroom in someone's home. Here, the signs seemed to be pointing in the other direction. The basket of amenities reminded me that this was a bedroom in a private apartment that was *simulating* a bedroom at a boutique hotel or inn.[10]

Economizing

The kitchen was down the hallway to the right, and when I arrived there in the morning at the appointed time Gretchen was waiting for me, dressed for work. She had already set the table for me, with a stylized white plate and bowl and shiny silverware. After an exchange of courtesies, she pointed out a thermos that she had filled with hot coffee, and explained how to use the coffeemaker to brew more if I wanted. I thanked her and said that I probably would not need more coffee. There was a fruit bowl with bananas, oranges and peaches, and she offered me a banana. Also on the table was a plastic container of yogurt—the generic brand from the discount supermarket, Aldi.

"If you would like to buy groceries," she said, "you can store them on the top shelf of the refrigerator." The refrigerator was half the size of a typical fridge in the United States. I was grateful for her generosity.

She placed her hand on the 500-gram yogurt container and told me that "each morning, you can have this much," pointing with her index finger to an imaginary line that was roughly two-thirds from the top. As the container was twelve inches high, she evidently thought it was fair that I consume about four inches' worth of yogurt. I recognized this gesture as expressing the value of economizing, of setting the limits of her generosity.

At Herr Klaus's inn I could either respect this boundary or eat more than he thought was appropriate. At Gretchen's, because it was a private apartment and I had a shelf in the refrigerator, I had the additional option of buying extra yogurt. And that was what I did—a container cost about one U.S. dollar, less than half of what I would have paid in the United States. I bought some fruit as well. But I was careful not to buy too much, knowing that if the fruit bowl attracted flies, I would have been to blame.

Mutual Online Feedback

Unlike Herr Klaus and other innkeepers, Gretchen, as an Airbnb hostess, did not need or seek recognition from the state authorities or, for that matter, any civic body, such as the local tourist office. Instead, for her, as indeed for me too, Airbnb itself created an authoritative realm to whose rules and regulations we dutifully deferred. Airbnb gains such power by framing and constraining the interaction of hosts and guests from beginning to end. After each stay, Airbnb sends both guests and hosts an email requesting that they give feedback to each other. The portion of the feedback that is made public as part of one's profile can contain words of advice, and thus can be associated with the primary value of giving advice that I previously identified as informing the practice of hospitality.

Herr Klaus was not subject to an Airbnb-style rating mechanism, so he could integrate a certain degree of hostility into his interaction with guests without fear of repercussions. Indeed, before the emergence of the Internet and the sharing economy, guests did not have many ways to censor hosts who had disappointed their expectations. They might call their travel agent or the local tourist office, or write to the publisher of the tourist guidebook that had featured the host. Similarly, innkeepers did not rate their guests; they could not readily shape their guests' reputations or influence how easily they could secure hospitality from other innkeepers in the future. Innkeepers and their guests could call on local authorities for help, but only in extreme cases.

In contrast, Airbnb's rating mechanism intrudes into the private lives of hosts, and to a lesser extent the lives of their guests, far more than travel agencies, local tourist offices, and guidebooks ever have. Airbnb's rating mechanism is also more all-encompassing than the systems used by websites such as TripAdvisor.com that rely on user-generated content to rate hotels and other travel-related venues, because the latter do not allow the travel establishments to rate guests. Since a bad review on Airbnb can limit the ability of hosts and guests to extend hospitality and receive it, respectively, the rating mechanism likely has some impact on the interaction of guests and hosts, including on the breadth of advice that hosts might dispense in person to their guests.

Within this constrained realm, hosts and guests can still act and interact in richly significant ways. Thus, for instance, my purchasing yogurt and fruit was an implicit critique of Gretchen's bounded generosity. This act of retaliation on my part was made possible partly by the fact that I was being hosted in a private apartment and had kitchen privileges. Needless to say, buying yogurt and fruit would not have constituted the same form of delicate retaliation at an inn, because bringing purchased provisions to an inn would come across as much more aggressive, even hostile. I expected Gretchen to notice the criticism that my purchases of yogurt and fruit implied, yet I hoped that she would focus more intently on another possible interpretation of my act, that it was an expression of generosity. I still wanted to make a favorable impression and predispose my hostess to leave a positive comment on my Airbnb profile. Indeed, besides bringing this gift of food, I made every effort to clean up after myself—loading the dishes into the small dishwasher, wiping the floor and sink in the bathroom, and generally going well beyond what I considered to be common courtesy at an inn, where cleaning is among the host's maintenance responsibilities.

Similarly, the tasteful décor at Gretchen's apartment could be interpreted, in part, as a strategy to attract notice and praise on Airbnb's website. Indeed, reading her profile on Airbnb, I saw that guests praised her for her good taste. Like these guests, I sat at the kitchen table and I admired the way she had decorated the kitchen, with a blue-and-white color scheme. The pot had a blue top, but the knob was white; a tea set in the same colors was displayed on a blue tray on a counter by the window. The blue box on top of the cabinet had white stripes, and the towels and other accessories were all aesthetically consistent.[11]

The Fantasy of Hosts' Advice

Airbnb's feedback mechanism, which is a manifestation of the practice of advising, extends to both hosts and guests. At Herr Klaus's, advising was the prerogative of the host, not the guest, and it mainly consisted of imparting information about local points of interest. With the advent of the Internet, guests are far less dependent on their hosts for basic information about an inn's environment than they used to be. Guests can use their mobile devices to access interactive maps that tell them precisely how to reach local points of interest. With information about locations, prices and operating hours so easily available, guests do not need their hosts to provide extra maps and verbal instructions.

This is not to say, however, that Airbnb deprives hosts of their advisory role. Rather, the Airbnb model shifts this role to a more local, personal, even intimate plane by emphasizing that a host's nuanced knowledge of local points of interest is especially valuable. On a previous version of Airbnb's website, one scrolled past information titled "Hospitality Standards" to a section titled "Personality." The subheading was: "Airbnb is made up of magical moments and hosts like you create them.

Let the personality of you and your listing transform the trip experience" (Airbnb n.d.a). Further down, Airbnb shared three points of advice, each dramatized by a photo:

> No one knows your space, your neighborhood, or your city like you do. Share your favorite places with them and introduce them to your closest pals.
>
> Guests often relish unconventional travel opportunities. Teach them something local and unforgettable.
>
> You invited your guest in...now consider inviting them out! Ask your guest if they would like to join you at your favorite cafe, museum, or neighborhood lounge.[12]

The advice targets hosts, urging them to share their knowledge with their guests.

It was notable that Gretchen did not share any local information with me on the morning after my arrival, aside from telling me how to reach the discount supermarket, Aldi. She may have refrained from offering expert advice because I had told her that I had lived in Leipzig before, and that the purpose of my visit was to do research at the Rosa Luxemburg Foundation.

Nevertheless, encountering content on Airbnb's website about hosts' advisory role conjures a fantasy of inclusion and belonging. As other commentators have noted, "experiencing a city and living like a local are valued and sought after by Airbnb users." (Yannopoulou et al. 2013: 88). The guidelines for hosts on Airbnb's website, then, can be viewed as having a promotional value. They bring to mind the possibility that one will experience the full promise of Airbnb on some future stay.

The Host as World Traveler

With its old writing desk and bookshelf, the bedroom doubled as a study, and judging from the small collection of books that my hostess made available to her guests, she preferred literary novels. She had an old copy of *The Little Prince*, published in East Berlin, and standing upright on the bookcase, facing the room, was a photo album of Leipzig during World War II. This book compared sites in Leipzig before and after the World War II Allied bombing campaigns. By prominently displaying this book, Gretchen, it seemed, wanted her guests to take notice of it. Half of Leipzig was destroyed in the war, and the book's photos featured many beautiful buildings that had been lost. Perhaps all she intended to show was how Leipzig had recovered. Yet as a guest from the United States, I could interpret the placement of this book as a statement about my country's shared responsibility for the devastation of the city that I was now visiting as a guest. Some guests might have reacted angrily to such a provocation, rejecting what the book's presence implied.

Both reactions, but particularly the former, have strong resonance in the German context: should people personally identify with a nation-state? Allegiance to the Third Reich brought death and destruction. West Germans' rejection of displays of national pride is, to a large extent, a consequence of World War II. The deeper message is also consistent with the collapse of East Germany, which made strange and problematic any continued identification with the symbolic artifacts of the socialist state. States create and break alliances, go to war and make peace in a multilayered drama of tragedy and repair that plays out at the individual and group levels. In the context of Airbnb, the photo album implied that people can strive to transcend the painful gyrations of international relations, and that Airbnb is a step in that direction.

This implied message, along with Gretchen's disclosure of her recent visit to the pilgrimage route of Santiago de Compostela and the art from India that decorated the bedroom walls, suggested that my hostess wished to be seen as cosmopolitan. The interior décor of inns often contains elements that refer to the immediate region, including local landmarks. These token reminders of the local culture create a distance between guests who arrive from elsewhere and the inn's proprietors. Gretchen's apartment did not follow this convention. As a guest from abroad, I fit right in with the other foreign artifacts. My presence, and my knowledge of the presence of previous guests, enhanced my impression of the apartment's cosmopolitan character. Rather than accentuate a preexisting contrast between foreign and local, my presence affirmed my hostess's interest in foreign travel.

BEING A HOST AND A GUEST CONCURRENTLY

Guests and hosts mutually constitute each other's identity. For Herr Klaus, successfully managing and containing one's guests affirmed his identity as a host. For Gretchen, hosting through Airbnb was a source of additional income, contributing to her ability to travel. The guest's presence alluded to her past and future travel, and the guest's identity as a tourist and traveler mirrored her own lifestyle choices and aspirations. For innkeepers of Herr Klaus's generation, opportunity for foreign travel was very limited, and this sort of mirroring was impossible.

One Airbnb video, available on YouTube, directly builds on the equivalence of guest and host. "How To Airbnb" [sic] (with German subtitles, it is titled "So funktioniert Airbnb!") features a narrator who first introduces the concept of Airbnb through her experiences as a guest.[13] Then, a little over a minute into the video, she switches sides, so to speak, and introduces herself in another guise, that of an Airbnb hostess. She says, "When I'm out of town, I put my place on Airbnb." The video frame shows a yellow card leaning on a wine bottle with the words, "Loved the place!" The narrator picks up this yellow card, and we see the bottle on a table next to a key on a keychain. In the next frame, the camera zooms out to reveal the narrator standing next to the same table. She wears a coat and holds a suitcase. Presumably, she has just returned home. Hanging on the door in the back is a magenta-colored sign that says, "$90 Per Night." She explains, "It helps me pay for all my adventures and lets me treat myself to something special once in a while."

I infer from this scene that while she was away on an adventure, during which she stayed at an Airbnb, she rented out her own space through Airbnb for ninety U.S. dollars a night. Her guests liked her place so much that they left for her a bottle wine as a gift.[14] The more basic message, however, is that hosts can be guests, and guests hosts, and that they can even inhabit these two roles simultaneously.

The idea that a person can be concurrently a guest and a host is not unique to Airbnb: print media, such as university alumni magazines, have been facilitating peer-to-peer housing exchange for decades, if not longer. But Airbnb has expanded the scope of such exchanges, extending them beyond immediate reciprocity and into a transaction that involves three interlinked parties: the hosts are not the guests of their guests, but guests of some other hosts. In this sense and others, Airbnb is often considered to be a prime example of the peer-to-peer economy (Sundararajan 2014: 6), with the word "peer" conjuring the interaction within a symmetrical dyad, or pair of equals. In the conclusion of the first part of this book, I mentioned the complementary roles that form the basis of social institutions—in education, the student and the teacher; in medicine, the caregiver and the patient; in the workplace, the employer and the employee. The peer-to-peer dyad implies a certain identity or interchangeability, whereby each individual is potentially in a position to perform the role of the other.

In later sections of this book, I will examine what the resemblance between hosts and guests can tell us about the power dynamics between them. Here I would like to point out that the blending of the two identities is also a focus of organizational learning. Airbnb's CEO "sees the company expanding its effort to educate hosts," an effort that includes the creation of a "Hospitality Lab in Dublin" and "additional e-learning software for hosts" (MacMillan 2013). The Airbnb app allows hosts to join other hosts in online groups, where they can "give each other tips on what worked" (MacMillan 2013). Hosts learn how to be better hosts by playing the role of guests; indeed, one of the goals of the Airbnb video is to encourage hosts to experience themselves as guests. Experiencing oneself as a guest is also seen as a learning tool for Airbnb executives (MacMillan 2013).

Reducing the distance between hosts and guests can be a challenging corporate learning prerogative. According to one manager at the Four Seasons, "We need employees who are as distinguished as our guests. If employees are going to adapt, to be empathetic and anticipate guest needs, the 'distance' between the employee and the guest has to be small" (Hallowell, Bowen and Knoop 2002: 8). Yet in the context of a hotel chain such as Four Seasons, the economic disparities between hosts and guests can be stark. In contrast, Airbnb hosts and guests are likely to mirror each other's travel consumption habits. Unlike a hotel employee, Gretchen used her hosting to supplement her primary income. Indeed, having a spare room to rent out marks her and other Airbnb hosts as relatively privileged. It is easy to imagine her and other Airbnb hosts translating their earnings from Airbnb into travel experiences, and then leveraging these experiences to become better hosts.

ARE GUESTS EQUAL TO HOSTS?

Representations of guests and hosts as identical or similar to one another often include assumptions about the balance of power between them. Maurice Hocart, an anthropologist active in the first decades of the twentieth century who examined hospitality across time and cultures, assumes that the guest's superiority is obvious to the point that people do not notice the need to explain it. He argued that the guest's superior power is grounded in the belief that the guest is divine (Hocart 1952: 78–86). Guests have the "power to confer life," a quality that is usually associated with divine beings (Raglan 1952: 7). "The divine patronage of the stranger," he contended, should be explained just as physicists are called to account for the fact that objects fall to the ground (Hocart 1952: 79).

I can discern echoes of Hocart in the abovementioned video "How To Airbnb" (Airbnb 2011a). In the video, the guests appear to be the more powerful party. The narrator's guests help finance her travel. The superiority of the guests is further communicated by their gift of wine. Wine connotes many meanings, including vitality; to follow Hocart, giving wine implies that guests have the power to confer life. The bottle of wine also demonstrates that the guests' reach extends beyond the monetary value of the exchange, and puts the hostess in their debt.

But the superiority of guests is not a given. For example, the image of the wine bottle in the video hints at the possibility that there might have been an original bottle, one that she, as a hostess, had left for her guests. If this is the case, then the bottle featured in the video is the gift that the guests have purchased for her in gratitude for her original gesture of generosity. This more complicated, but plausible, interpretation implies that the hostess is superior. It also conjures an exchange that blends the identities of guests and hosts. The guests consume their hosts' gift, and the hosts consume the guests' return gift.

The relative power of hosts and guests is a matter of concern to Brian Chesky, Airbnb's co-founder and CEO. Chesky has suggested that Airbnb seeks to empower hosts so that they are better at serving guests. He writes, "Dublin will be where we create our Hospitality Innovation Lab. Here, we will innovate on the customer experience. Our focus will be how to empower our hosts to provide excellent hospitality" (Chesky 2013). While his statement implies that guests are superior, Chesky melds the identities of host and guest, as did the narrator in the video. He explains that the purpose of the company's "European Customer Experience team" is to ensure "that your trip goes delightfully smooth, and your hosting is successful" (Chesky 2013). The second-person pronoun that he repeats, first addressing guests and then hosts, suggests that the readers of his blog entry, his audience, actually play both roles.

THE SPATIAL ASPECT OF THE GUESTS' SUPERIORITY

The anthropologist Maurice Hocart attributes much greater power to guests than to hosts. Yet he also notes that in ancient Greece, the same term was used for hosts and guests (Hocart 1952: 78; a similar ambiguity is found in German, see Seebold 2002: 332). He does not explore the contradictory implications of these two ideas. Operating in an economic and social context that Hocart could likely not imagine, Airbnb hosts and guests resemble each other, while at the same time, Airbnb still constitutes guests as the more powerful party. This is a tension worth exploring, first in the context of the anthropology of hospitality, and then with reference to the well-publicized recent criticism of Airbnb that is exerting particular pressure on hosts.

The relative strength of guests is a common theme in the anthropology of hospitality. Where anthropologists identify the hosts as the more powerful party, this is generally due to their greater control and knowledge of the immediate environment in which they extend hospitality to their guests. But with respect to the larger social space, anthropologists tend to attribute more power to guests (except when the hosts are members of an elite).

The power dynamics between hosts and guests are a function of social space. For example, drawing on his fieldwork in Uzbekistan, Russell Zanca writes about the sentiments of guests who yielded to their hosts' aggressive hospitality. In the immediate context of hospitality, the hosts have the upper hand. "Neophytes to the culture often overeat because they think it pleases the host and also because they think no other choice is left them" (2003: 14). But expatriates, for the most part, have more resources than their local Uzbek hosts. In the greater scheme of things, they are more powerful than their hosts.

In northern Pakistan, poor famers extend hospitality in a manner that maintains their "self-esteem...in the face of the wealth and luxury of neighbouring Oriental civilizations" whose ethical premises they perceive to be wrong (Barth 1981: 107). The foreign guests "are made to recognize the sovereignty of local people" (107). Yet in the larger world, the foreign guests are more powerful than their local hosts.

Charles Lindholm provides one of the most insightful analyses of hospitality. In the Swat Valley in northern Pakistan, where he conducted fieldwork, "the relation between the host and the guest is the relation between controller and controlled. As such, it reflects the social order, which is a continual struggle for control" (1982: 235). He locates Pukhtun hospitality on the caring and nurturing side of "a dialectic between love and hate, union and separation, community and individual, that must find expression in every society" (273). Though controlling, hosts in Swat are emotionally needy; hospitality in Swat is an opportunity for hosts to express love in a society in which "trust, love, and intimacy are not found ... once the child has been weaned" (268).

This nuanced analysis of hosts' emotional needs shows hosts in that cultural context to be vulnerable, refining our understanding of the host's superiority in the narrow spatial domain in which hospitality takes place. Overall, however, the examples from Zanca, Barth, and Lindholm all inscribe inequality with reference to social space. The guests, and not the hosts, are affiliated with power structures that dominate a far wider space. Of course, when anthropologists consider hosts who are members of an elite, a different pattern emerges (see examples in Rugh 2009; Shryock 1997). Nevertheless, the examples that I have shared are part of a larger pattern. According to Erve Chambers, "anthropologists have tended to view tourism as a manifestation of international and mainly unequal relationships between tourists and their 'hosts.' They have given much less attention to domestic tourism or to touristic exchanges among social and economic peers" (2000: ix).[15]

Airbnb is a particularly interesting case because its hosts and guests so closely resemble each other.[16] At the same time, just as the previously discussed pattern suggests, Airbnb guests are at an advantage that has a spatial dimension. Airbnb is under scrutiny in New York, Frankfurt, and Berlin for the potentially negative impact it has on buildings and neighborhoods. Local authorities are exerting regulatory pressure on Airbnb and Airbnb hosts, creating a force field that gives an advantage to guests over hosts.

For example, two related sources of conflict—the evidence of which comes from New York City, but could easily surface in Leipzig—are safety and maintenance.[17] In some buildings, neighbors complain that when Airbnb guests are given a key to the front door of the building, it compromises security in the common areas. Airbnb guests raise the level of noise in the building, and with their luggage, increase the wear and tear on communal hallways.[18]

Another source of conflict is Airbnb's impact on the availability of rental apartments. In some of Berlin's highly desirable neighborhoods, one out of fifty apartments is listed on Airbnb (Kotowski 2014b). Consequently, Berlin has imposed some legal restrictions on Airbnb (Hill 2015), although these measures have not been all that effective. There is a German website called Airbnb vs. Berlin, or www.airbnbvsberlin.de, that depicts Airbnb's activities in the housing market in Berlin through graphs. The website states that despite legal restrictions, the data show that Airbnb is having a significant impact on some neighbor-hoods, implying that it depletes the housing stock to the detriment of would-be renters and buyers. Most recently, Berlin has imposed "fines of up to 100,000 Euros," which, if enforced, would deter Airbnb hosts from turning apartments into vacation homes for Airbnb guests (Kim 2016). Similarly, Frankfurt, which with 821 Airbnb listings ranks just above Leipzig,[19] has issued laws regulating Airbnb, making it illegal for owners to turn their apartments into vacation homes (Kotowski 2014a).

It is important to acknowledge in this regard that a considerable number of Airbnb hosts are not "regular people" but "professional land-lords and property managers" (Hill 2015). Three of the largest property owners in the U.S., "Equity Residential, AvalonBay Communities Inc. and Camden Property Trust...are interested in pursuing a revenue-sharing model with Airbnb" (Kusisto 2015). These types of hosts are attracted by the fact that rental apartments that are converted to de facto hotels fetch a high rate of return (Hill 2015). These large property owners might wish to collaborate with Airbnb and with tenants who wish to be Airbnb hosts.

I envision future research on these and other potential conflict areas for Airbnb in Leipzig. Starting from the ground up, the researcher could examine how different stakeholders in Leipzig talk about Airbnb. Even in the absence of overt conflict in Leipzig between Airbnb and housing advocates, city hall administrators, politicians and other stakeholders, awareness that tensions exist in other cities could lead hosts to suspect that their Airbnb-related work would, at some point, clash with local norms and values, making them more cautious in their interactions with guests than otherwise would have been the case.[20] The conflict between local authorities and Airbnb spatially encodes an advantage for Airbnb guests over hosts. In a manner that recalls examples from the anthropol-ogy of hospitality, the emergence of these fault lines between Airbnb and municipal authorities suggest that in certain social arenas outside the immediate household in which the hospitality is taking place, the status of Airbnb hosts is more precarious than that of their guests.

Interestingly, the power dynamics between hosts and guests are also modulated by Airbnb itself. If the previous examples pertain to the spatial dimensions of relative power, the following examples pertain to its tem-poral dimension. Airbnb orchestrates the power difference between hosts and guests in a predetermined sequence, harnessing time to create accountability and give the advantage to guests.

Harnessing Time to Create Accountability

In the introduction to the first part of this book, I differentiate between hospitality as friendly and inclusive sociability (*Gastfreundschaft*), and hospitality as a service-like interaction (*Gastlichkeit*) (Pechlaner and Raich 2007: 14, 17). Because Airbnb is a "broker" of hospitality, its imprint is, in large measure, managerial in nature. It organizes and facilitates the interaction of hosts and guests, a function previously fulfilled by guidebooks, travel agencies, and tourist offices. Like other businesses within the sharing economy, Airbnb's website carefully orchestrates the interaction between hosts and guests in a temporal sequence, with the final step being feedback: after the visit, the parties have two weeks to submit comments on their experience. They do not have access to each other's feedback until this two-week period has elapsed.

This final round of feedback always has the potential to turn hostile, which puts both hosts and guests in a vulnerable position. Each party is at risk of receiving an unfair or demeaning comment that would diminish its reputation. At the same time, the wish for a positive review, and the desire to avoid a negative one, motivates hosts and guests alike to be on their best behavior and avoid actions that might be interpreted as hostile. As such, the feedback mechanism represents a significant departure from pre-Internet practices of hospitality, especially traditions of hospitality that allow hosts to express a measure of hostility toward their guests.

The night before my departure, I left the door to my room open; when I saw Gretchen walk by, I stepped into the hallway and started a conversation. I told her that I was leaving the next day, and thanked her for the stay. She said that I was very quiet, a comment that I interpreted as shifting the responsibility for our limited contact to me. Approximately a day after I left Gretchen's apartment, I received an email from Airbnb informing me that I had two weeks to leave feedback about my stay. I presumed that Gretchen had received a similar email from Airbnb.[21]

Both of us, I could confidently assume, were seeking a positive review. After all, negative feedback from past hosts could prevent guests from accessing hospitality through Airbnb in the future. For hosts who are eager to supplement their income through Airbnb, the stakes are particularly high, because a bad review, justified or unjustified, could jeopardize their ability to attract guests.

Compromised Accountability

Airbnb ordains a schedule that, in predetermined fashion, makes hosts more vulnerable than guests. Over time, hosts either gain or lose in reputation, making them more or less able to attract future guests. For example, commenting on an article that compares the ratings of accommodations that are listed on Airbnb and TripAdvisor, one Airbnb hostess writes:

> Airbnb send you a nasty note if you get two four-star ratings in a row and will drop you if you get three. So, the premise of this paper is totally flawed, as hotels do not automatically go out of business when their trip advisor ratings go below some random minimum [sic].[22]

While the consequences of receiving a two-star rating three times in a row may or may not be as harsh this Airbnb hostess claims, her post conveys her feelings of powerlessness and frustration. Indeed, fearful of a bad review,

> Hosts may take great pains to avoid negative reviews, ranging from rejecting guests that they deem unsuitable, to pre-empting a suspected negative review with a positive 'pre-ciprocal' review, to resetting a property's reputation with a fresh property page when a property receives too many negative reviews [sic].[23]

Because the stakes are high for both hosts and guests, participants "often refrain from leaving a critiqued review unless it was just truly, truly an awful experience" [sic] (Ho 2015). Perhaps to correct this problem, Airbnb allows for private feedback in addition to the feedback that becomes part of one's public record on Airbnb's website. According to Emil Protalinski (2014), Airbnb allows guests—and guests only—to leave confidential feedback for hosts in the form of a private email through Airbnb's website, in addition to the regular option of leaving a comment on a host's public profile.[24] Protalinski's observation, though now outdated, confirms Airbnb's preference for empowering guests over hosts. More recently, Erica Ho notes that Airbnb now allows both hosts and guests the option of leaving each other private feedback:

> The company furthered altered their review policy to let hosts and guests leave both public and private feedback simultaneously. While it lets hosts/

guests see what can be improved upon during the experience, it significantly minimizes the amount of public negative feedback. Both hosts and guests feel freer to comment honestly, but the thing is that it all happens **behind closed doors with no accountability** that the issue will be fixed in the future. There is no transparency for future host/guests, who are forking over their cash or their home [sic, emphasis in the original].[25]

If individuals are leaving positive feedback on each other's public profiles, then this is beneficial to Airbnb. "The 'testimonials' are a critical feature of the website, and help construct the brand as warm and human" (Yannopoulou et al. 2013: 88). The "references to friendship, love, homeliness, and gift-giving" in the feedback field suggest that the same positive attributes apply to Airbnb (88).

Yet to follow Erica Ho, allowing hosts and guests to keep some of their written feedback to each other private contradicts the broader goal of making hosts and guests accountable. Nested within this dilemma is the question of Airbnb's own accountability. It is likely that many visitors to Airbnb's website do not know that hosts and guests can bypass the public profile feature and give each other feedback through Airbnb's website that other hosts and guests will not be able to view. This lack of transparency compromises Airbnb's own accountability to hosts, guests, and other stakeholders.

WHEN HOSPITALITY FAILS

Airbnb's rating mechanism allows it to attract, retain, and reward the right hosts and guests. Most Airbnb hosts and guests would likely agree with these prerogatives, as well as Airbnb's disciplining, and if necessary removing, bad hosts and guests from its network. After all, given a choice, most people would prefer to avoid guests or hosts who transgress the norms of hospitality. While some traditions of hospitality can accommodate a measure of host-guest hostility, all hospitality practices have a breaking point. The pervasiveness of stories in anthropology and other sources in which hospitality breaks down suggests that it was just a matter of time before some very disappointing Airbnb visits would be retold as examples of failed hospitality. The popular media refers to such Airbnb visits as "Airbnb horror stories." Indeed, as the title of a recent news story—"Airbnb horror stories are the new internet meme"—suggests, bloggers and other content creators on the Internet use the idea of "horror" to imagine hospitality breakdowns in the context of Airbnb.[26] Similarly, typing into the Google search field "Airbnb ho" prompts Google to autocomplete the search string "Airbnb horror story."[27]

One important source of Airbnb horror stories on the Internet is www.AirbnbHell.com, a website that "is dedicated to helping hosts and guests spread the word about the risks and dangers of using Airbnb." The tabs "Guest Stories" and "Host Stories" feature 25 horror stories each, with links to additional stories. This numerical balance suggests that this website attributes the potential to do harm equally to guests and hosts. While it would take a deeper analysis to discern whether one party actually tends to be more at fault than the other, the website's message is that Airbnb itself is really to blame for these bad outcomes. Indeed, the www.AirbnbHell.com homepage provides a "list of reasons why you should NOT use Airbnb" that details the ways in which Airbnb fails to protect both guests and hosts.

While sometimes it is the hosts and at other times the guests that are immediately at fault, the one constant theme in Airbnb horror stories is Airbnb's lack of accountability. Even more crucially, hospitality horror stories offer insight into the power dynamics between hosts and guests.[28] As an initial step in exploring this source material, I share in the following pages stories of failed hospitality in diverse contexts, including Airbnb. I organize these stories by noting the source or cause of the disruption. I find that breakdowns in hospitality tend to emerge: (1) from the setting in which it is supposed to take place; (2) in the initial encounter, when hosts and guests are still strangers to each other; (3) in the course of host-guest interaction; and (4) after the guests and hosts part ways, when the reputation of one party or both parties is unfairly diminished or even destroyed. I will first draw on this four-part framework to categorize the incidents in which hospitality breaks down, and then, in the section that follows, I will attempt to define what "horror" means in the context of Airbnb, and shed light on the way in which Airbnb hosts and guests mutually construct each other.

(1) *The setting.* The setting is an important factor in many hospitality horror stories, most famously when a hotel or an inn's unique history leads to the suspension of ordinary social bonds. "Whilst the hotel is subject to the same laws and mores which govern our lives elsewhere, it is also seemingly a place of anonymity where guests can 'disappear' and where the normal social conventions can be challenged and flouted" (Pritchard and Morgan 2006: 764). Two well-known fictional depictions of such a

setting are Hitchcock's film *Psycho* (which was originally a book by Robert Bloch) and Stephen King's novel *The Shining* (which was later made into a film). These hotels are sites of "transgressive behaviour" that are associated with other liminal places, such as crossroads, "magical places and traditional sites of hangmen's gibbets" (764). In Germany, for example, the *Nobiskrug* is a pub or inn of low repute in a border area. Historically attracting customs officials and smugglers as patrons, it is traditionally associated with hell, imagined as a place where the dead can carouse until the Last Judgment (Wallner 1968: 31–32).

The Airbnb horror stories that I found do not conjure the supernatural in the manner of the previous examples. Instead, they report on accidents and unexpected inconveniences. In Zak Stone's article about his father's death at an Airbnb, a rope swing that seemed safe proved fatal (2015). Morgan Joyce reports on two less serious set of incidents, one in which she was sick but had no access to a toilet, and another in which she fell ill because the heating system was broken and she was cold (2016).

(2) *The initial encounter.* Hospitality horror stories also arise in connection with the initial encounter between prospective hosts and guests, when they are still strangers to each other—the moment when the locals decide whether or not to extend hospitality, assume the role of hosts, and impute to the arriving strangers the status of guests. For example, in travelogues written by early European traders and sailors in Oceania, it is reported that locals sometimes saw arriving strangers as "'long pig' (human flesh to eat)," and at other times received them as guests (Campbell 1981: 34). Traders and sailors whom locals classified as "long pig" (34) were killed, dismembered, cooked, and eaten.

In one story, a woman assumed the identity of a guest as a ruse to enter a home, and was caught on the home's security camera "stealing over 35,000 dollars in valuables."[29] In another story—one in which the encounter between host and guest was entirely virtual—the guest, Sonia, was looking forward to attending a series of Formula One events in Austin, Texas, and booked a local Airbnb many months in advance. The subtitle to her account is a good summary of what happened next: "The story of how Airbnb allowed a host to triple the rate and cancel my reservation after an agreement had been made." Sonia levels this charge at Airbnb: "I find it shocking that Airbnb doesn't have a mechanism in place to prevent this type of scenario and to protect both parties" (Fulton 2015; Sonia 2014).[30]

(3) *During the visit.* Third, hospitality horror stories can emerge during a visit. Many of the examples that Andrew Shryock has collected involve the host offering food to the guest—and then murdering him (2012: S25–S26).

> I have seen that things are likely to go wrong when a shift in political scale is attempted, when a host tries to reduce his equals to the status of guests, or subordinates assert their status as hosts. These moments are rich in potential for disaster, largely because a claim to sovereignty is being made before a new house has been completely built, or a rival house has been completely demolished.[31]

Another well-known example of failed hospitality that has been much discussed in anthropology is Captain Cook's visit to Hawaii. At first treated as an honored guest, he later became the target of hostile action by natives that resulted in his death. The circumstances leading to his death have been discussed in the context of a rich debate in anthropology about the worldview of different sectors of Hawaiian society (Borofsky 1997). While I do not wish to sidestep this important and complex debate, it is interesting to conceive of Captain Cook's fate in Hawaii as a hospitality horror story, one in which the horror was foreshadowed in the very offer of hospitality: Captain Cook's host apparently had hoped that Captain Cook, after having been given a sumptuous welcome, would "reciprocate with military assistance against Maui" (Kane 1997: 265).

In Airbnb horror stories, too, the horror sometimes emerges during the stay. In some stories, an individual suddenly abandons the role of host or guest in order to harm the other party. For example, in a story featured on many websites, an Airbnb hostess in Madrid was accused of locking a young man visiting from Massachusetts inside her apartment and sexually assaulting him (Lieber 2015). In another story, an Airbnb host showed up in the middle of the night and started to harass his guests (Fulton 2015; Bort 2014).

(4) *After the stay.* Lastly, in some cases hospitality failure occurs after a stay, when either a host or a guest diminishes the other party's reputation. According to Russell Zanca, expatriates in Uzbekistan who do not know how to refuse their hosts' offers of food and thus end up overeating sometimes employ "tabloid-style headline remarks" when they speak about their experiences with local hosts, "including 'culinary terrorism,' 'force feasting,' 'torture the guest,' and 'Hellspitality'" (Zanca 2003: 14). Of course, the very

hosts whom the expatriates decry likely fear the social stigma and isolation associated with having the reputation of being bad hosts (9). In some highly ritualized traditions of hospitality, aspects of the ritual refer directly to the parties' anxiety over their reputations. Among certain Bedouins in Jordan, the ritual of hospitality features four cups of coffee. The first cup is drunk by the host, who "leaves [a] few drops in this first cup for the guest to drink. By doing so, the guest would preserve his own reputation and that of the host" [sic] (al-'Abbadi quoted in Shryock 2004: 37).

All Airbnb horror stories can be classified as examples of this fourth type of hospitality failure, insofar as the individuals involved are hurt or embarrassed by the negative publicity. There is, however, also a special class of Airbnb horror stories in which the moment of failure occurs only after the visit has taken place, in the form of a damning review. The hosts in the following example refused their guests' request for a partial refund, and later found their reputation under attack. The guests

> decided to get back at us and slander us with a bunch of false claims in the review. I called Airbnb and told them that there clearly was no indication of our unit being in bad condition and that it was apparent the only time things got ugly was after we denied the refund.[32]

Airbnb acknowledges on its website that there is a risk of its rating mechanism being misused. On a page titled "What is Airbnb's Extortion Policy?" Airbnb states that "any attempt to use reviews to force a user to do something they aren't obligated to do is a misuse of reviews, and we don't allow it" (Airbnb n.d.b). For some guests, misleading information on a host's Airbnb profile precipitated an Airbnb horror story. For example, the author of "A Staycay Turned Sour: Our Airbnb Horror Story" was upset that previous guests left a positive review of the property that she had visited and found disappointing (Wordweed 2016).

In the previous examples, and in other Airbnb horror stories, Airbnb is blamed for not preventing crises, and for not taking the right corrective measures when the crises occur. Having developed a network of hosts and guests, Airbnb is held responsible for these deeply disappointing experiences. But there is more to be learned from examples of failed hospitality, from the distinct ways in which hospitality fails in the context of Airbnb, and from the connection between these incidents and our idea of "horror." What can all this teach us about the relationship between hosts and guests?

What Can Fail?

There is, of course, a big gap between disappointment and horror, and indeed the label "horror" should not be taken too literally. Nevertheless, incidents of hospitality failure, within Airbnb's network and beyond, are instructive in that they show guests and hosts stepping out of their respective roles and precipitating a social drama that puts an end to hospitality. When the failure is in the setting, the guests might remain on the premises but feel compelled to assume responsibilities that they perceive to be their hosts'. In some stories of breakdown, one party intentionally betrays the other, and in others the breakdown is due to negligence or incompetence.

Failed hospitality is sometimes linked to extreme hostility, but interestingly, this is not always so. In the first part of this book, I showed that Herr Klaus remained true to the values of economizing, advising, and allying himself with local authorities even while expressing hostility toward his guest. I argued that traditions of hospitality that integrate hostility are likely to be more resilient than traditions of hospitality in which hosts must be generous and always protect their guests. In contrast, failed hospitality is fundamentally the result of strangers reneging on their own identity claims and violating the integrity of the host-guest dyad.

While my framework emphasizes principles that are shared across different traditions of hospitality, it is logical to assume that each tradition of hospitality would be associated with a unique set of incidents of failure, and that analyzing these specific forms of failure would yield a richer understanding of each unique tradition of hospitality that they violate. As one might expect, Airbnb horror stories often emphasize flawed and frustrated attempts to communicate with the other party (Fulton 2015; Bort 2014; Sonia 2014). In such circumstances, the hosts and the guests cease to mirror each other, dashing any expectation of mutual resemblance and affinity.

Indeed, it is perhaps the expectation that Airbnb hosts and guests mirror each other that best explains the correlation between stories of Airbnb hospitality failure and the metaphor of horror. "Horror" captures the heightened experience of disappointment, anger, and helplessness that arise when the mirror is shattered. The guests might encounter a serious flaw in their accommodations, a flaw that they would never have imposed on their guests if they were the hosts. Or hosts or guests might discover that the other party has unexpectedly assumed a different, outside role and is attempting to frame their interaction with respect to a set of rules with which they do not agree, and which they themselves would never have imposed on the other party had they played the reverse role.[33]

CONCLUSION

One potential subject for future research is the tension between hosts' and guests' experience of hospitality and Airbnb's representation of hospitality in promotional materials such as videos. These tensions would have to be explored carefully, as thematic continuity across contexts does not necessarily entail semantic continuity. An example of a successful treatment of a similar problem of semantic continuity across contexts is found in Andrew Shryock's study of hospitality in Jordan. Shryock examines "how images of 'house' and 'hospitality' are reshaped" when "hospitality is nationalized and rendered public" (2004: 37). His Bedouin informants note that hospitality is corrupted and misused when it is made to "belong to a social field that no longer includes 'real' hosts, guests, or houses" (40). In the second part of this book, I have explored the significance advising guests and allegiance to the authorities. I have also examined the power dynamics between hosts and guests, their seeming resemblance, their mutual vulnerability, representations of failed hospitality, and the significance of hostility in hospitality. I investigated these themes across distinct contexts: my stay at Gretchen's, cases from the anthropological record from around the world, and recent "Airbnb horror stories" from North America and Europe. While more careful contextualization than I have provided here would likely have yielded a more nuanced understanding of these phenomena, as a whole, the resulting pattern yields a meaningful contrast to Herr Klaus's hospitality.

Gretchen's practice of hospitality is partly an extension of Airbnb's platform. Through its website, Airbnb reconfigures the values of advising the guests and allegiance to local authorities. With respect to advising, Airbnb encourages hosts to direct their guests to attractions that only locals know about. Airbnb's rating mechanism displaces some of the functions previously fulfilled by local representatives of the law. Airbnb hosts are typically not registered with their city or government. They do not have a relationship with the local tourist office, or membership in a local trade group or hospitality-related association. Airbnb profiles serve to communicate the identities of the hosts and guests, and Airbnb facilitates the financial transactions between them, obviating the need for hosts to collect payment directly from their guests. The online platform also allows hosts and guests to rate each other for the benefit of future guests and hosts, and to give each other feedback. While the rating mechanism helps prevent incidents of disappointment and failed hospitality—failures to which some media give the sensational label "Airbnb horror stories"—online reviews also put hosts and guests at risk of suffering unfair comments, reputation loss, diminished access to hospitality, and, in extreme cases, exclusion from Airbnb's network. This omnipresent danger, in turn, likely motivates hosts and guests to suppress any expression of overt hostility. Airbnb hosts and guests thus tend to conduct themselves in ways that fall on a continuum between social engagement, at one extreme, and social avoidance, at the other.

In contrast, Herr Klaus's behavior, as described in the first part of this book, always fell on a continuum between friendliness and hostility. He expressed his values of economizing and advising either to draw close to his guests or to distance himself from them.[34] In circumstances in which he was particularly vulnerable, he was hostile, which created social distance. His example could be adequately described by following a temporal and spatial movement from near to more distant contexts. I situated Herr Klaus in relation to his social position in pre- and post-communist Leipzig, to the fraying of the social safety net for East Germans after reunification, and then to the history of hospitality in East Germany and Germany as a whole. Then, drawing on examples of hospitality from other cultures, I speculated that traditions of hospitality that allow hosts to integrate hostility into their practices are more resilient than those which limit hosts to always being generous and protective toward their guests.

Gretchen's practice of hospitality—because it was an extension of Airbnb, a platform that can be accessed at any time and that constitutes an ever-present context in which I, as a guest, participated—would likely defy any attempt to locate it in a sequence of receding, nested spatial and temporal contexts.[35] This resistance to established modes of analysis, along with the fact that Airbnb is a new phenomenon, makes it more difficult for the anthropologist to step back and arrive at broad generalizations. Nevertheless, it is clear that through its online review system, Airbnb does allow hosts to express hostility, and guests to do the same. This capacity is likely a source of resilience, as well as added complexity, for the contemporary form of hospitality. The capacity to express hostility through the online review system is woven into the main themes that I encountered during my stay at Gretchen's apartment and in the course of my subsequent research: the resemblance between hosts and guests, horror, the fear of failed hospitality, and diminished allegiance to local authorities. I hope that my exploration of the surprising connections among these themes inspires future research into hospitality, the ancient but continually evolving relationship between hosts and their guests.

NOTES

1. MetroFocus 2016; Kotowski 2014a, b.
2. Arjun Appadurai conceptualizes the global flows of ideas, media and capital as "ideoscapes," "mediascapes," and "financescapes," respectively, arguably overstating the break between the present era of globalization and its historical antecedents and understating the decisive role of finance (Heyman and Campbell 2009: 132, 136). Others, such as Manuel Castells, relate flows to social networks (see Warf 2010: 2600). While one could draw on the example of Airbnb to explore these ideas, I do not follow this path here, as my purpose is to understand hospitality rather than contribute to a theory of globalization.
3. Stadt Leizpig, Amt für Statistik und Wahlen 1996: 37.
4. Stadt Leipzig 2016a.
5. There were 6253 births in Leipzig in 2015. See (Stadt Leipzig 2016b) and (Eberstadt 1994).
6. Stadt Leipzig 2016c.
7. Das Statistik-Portal 2016.
8. Here I identify three factors that might predispose Leipzig to be accepting of Airbnb. More research is needed on each of these factors.
9. I have changed my description of the artwork to protect the privacy of my hostess.
10. Yannopoulou, Moufahim, and Bian note that "innovativeness and authenticity are the key to Airbnb's identity" and connect these themes to the effort to seem businesslike: "Given the commercial nature of the exchange, great care is taken in constructing an image of efficiency and professionalism" (Yannopoulou et al. 2013: 89).
11. I changed the description of the kitchen to protect the privacy of my hostess.
12. Airbnb n.d.a. I found the same content points in German on Airbnb's German-language site, https://www.airbnb.de/hospitality.
13. Airbnb 2011a, b.
14. It should be noted that this gift is not in any way a tip, because a tip would imply that the host is a service professional, occupying a socially inferior role. More generally, tipping is a morally fraught issue in the history of hospitality and public education in Germany (more accurately, *nationalen Pädagogik*, or national pedagogy), going back to the

nineteenth century (Kämpfen 1975: 13). The jurist Ihering (more commonly referred to as Rudolf von Jhering, with a 'J') argued that tipping encourages vices like begging, greed, false or feigned friendship, vanity, and hedonism among service personnel (11). He wanted service people to be penalized for receiving tips, and employers to pay enough that tipping would not be necessary (14). The controversy about tipping continues (Taylor and Orenstein 2016).

More generally, Jhering saw the law not as a closed system, but as evolving in response to human purpose (Bond 2011). In his history of hospitality he argued that initially strangers had no legal rights. With the rise of trade, it became important to extend hospitality to strangers, and from this practical need emerged the customary feeling that one should extend hospitality to strangers (Jhering 1887: 397). Had I attempted to incorporate Jhering's history of hospitality into the first part of this book where I discuss this very same topic, I would have had difficulty reconciling his perspective with the perspective of the other authors that I have read.

15. While Chambers' point is instructive, his book is a seminal contribution to the anthropology of tourism, a field of study in which the word "hosts" refers to locals and migrant workers who serve guests, and the word "guests" refers to tourists. In contrast, I employ the word hosts to refer to innkeepers, Airbnb hosts, and hotel employees.

16. Anthropologists of tourism have been discussing the resemblance between hosts and guests for quite some time. Because they define hosts and guests more broadly than I do, our arguments do not perfectly overlap, a misalignment that merits a separate treatment at another point in time. But I want to mention here Theron Nuñez's argument that hosts, when faced with an onslaught of tourists year after year, may assume new identities and roles indicative of acculturation, a process in which they become more like their guests. Hosts, he writes, "become more like the tourists' culture" (1989: 266). And writing about Port Douglas in Queensland, Australia, Kirsty Sherlock approaches the topic from another angle. She explains that

> the blurred distinction between host and guest is created due to the complex flow of residents arriving and leaving again, with many returning periodically. Just under half (47 percent) of those surveyed intend to leave the town. Many of these indicated that they would be returning to Port Douglas as tourists to visit friends and relatives they were leaving behind. Thus, guests become hosts and hosts become guests over time. (Sherlock 2001: 277)

17. MetroFocus 2016.

18. MetroFocus 2016.
19. Das Statistik-Portal 2016.
20. Incidentally, knowledge of Airbnb's conflicts with regulators could also be a source of hosts' diminished allegiance to local authorities.
21. Because Airbnb profiles are public and, as an anthropologist, I am obligated to keep Gretchen's identity confidential, I do not share additional specifics.
22. Parachutewoman 2015.
23. Zervas et al. 2015: 12. The previous hostess, Parachutewoman, refers to this paper.
24. Protalinski 2014.
25. Ho 2015.
26. Armitage, November 12, 2015. Not all the situations that commentators call "horror stories" deserve this label. Scholars of discourse analysis in the Internet age may shed more light on this strong choice of words.
27. Sullivan, April 6, 2011.
28. "The guest's hostility is...a menacing consequence of his potential inter-changeability with the host" (McNulty 2007: xii). "Western literature and myth are full of legends that cast the relationship between the host and guest as potentially menacing" (xii).
29. ABC News 2015. Rather than using the label "horror" for its compilation of stories, ABC News employed the word "nightmare." One must be careful not to overlook a specific pattern of meaning, as "Airbnb horror stories" and "Airbnb nightmare stories" might diverge from each other in significant respects. I classify the "nightmare" stories reported by ABC News as examples of Airbnb horror stories.
30. I first encountered Sonia's story in Fulton (2015), where it was given as an example of an Airbnb horror story.
31. Shryock 2012: S25.
32. Anonymous 2016, published on AirbnbHell.com.
33. Literary theory offers a broader and deeper analysis of horror (see, for example, David Punter's *A New Companion to the Gothic*, 2012).
34. I do not have evidence of Herr Klaus expressing allegiance to local authorities as a means of drawing closer to his guests. I only have evidence of him doing so to create social distance.
35. It would be interesting to study Airbnb from the perspective of digital anthropology, while borrowing from Arjun Appadurai's theory of global flows (Heyman and Campbell 2009) and network theory. According to Manuel Castells, flows are "the expression of the processes dominating our economic, political, and symbolic life.... Thus, I propose the idea that there is a new spatial form characteristic of social practices that dominate and shape the network

society: The space of flows. The space of flows is the material organization of time-sharing social practices that work through flows. By flows I understand purposeful, repetitive, programmable sequences of exchange and interaction between physically disjointed positions held by social actors" [sic] (Castells in Warf 2010: 2600). It would be interesting to relate Airbnb's online network, which disrupts the familiar ordering of time and space, to Castells' abstract conceptualization of a network of physically distant actors.

REFERENCES

ABC News. 2015. Airnbnb Home Rental Nightmares. https://www.youtube.com/watch?v=PfDAEF02tp0. Published on Aug 6, 2015. Accessed January 18, 2016.

Airbnb. 2011a. How To Airbnb. https://www.youtube.com/watch?v=SaOFuW011G8. Published on January 5, 2011. Accessed December 29, 2015.

Airbnb. 2011b. So funktioniert Airbnb! https://www.youtube.com/watch?v=hueKmhNNI_Y. Published on May 4, 2011. Accessed December 28, 2015.

Airbnb. n.d.a. Personality. https://www.airbnb.com/hospitality. Accessed December 29, 2015.

Airbnb. n.d.b. What is Airbnb's Extortion Policy? https://www.airbnb.com/help/article/548/what-is-airbnb-s-extortion-policy?topic=253. Accessed April 20, 2016.

Airbnb. www.AirbnbHell.com. Accessed January 18, 2016.

Airbnb. http://www.airbnbvsberlin.de. Accessed May 4, 2016.

Anonymous. 2016. Even Airbnb SUPERHOSTS are treated like tools! In *AirbnbHell*. http://www.airbnbhell.com/even-airbnb-superhosts-treated-like-tools/. Published on February 4, 2016. Accessed April 3, 2016.

Armitage, Catherine. 2015. Airbnb Horror Stories are the New Internet Meme. http://www.smh.com.au/technology/technology-news/airbnb-horror-stories-are-the-new-internet-meme-20151111-gkwag4.html. Published on November 12, 2015. Accessed January 23, 2016.

Barth, Fredrik. 1981. Pathan Identity and its Maintenance. In *Features of Person and Society in Swat: Collected Essays on Pathans. Selected Essays of Fredrik Barth*. Vol. II, 103–120. London: Routledge and Kegan Paul and International Library of Anthropology.

Bond, Niall. 2011. The Displacement of Normative Discourse from Legal Theory to Empirical Sociology: Ferdinand Tönnies, Natural Law, the Historical School, Rudolf Von Jhering and Otto Von Gierke. *Forum Historiae Iuris (2011): Forum Historiae Iuris*, 1 September 2011. http://www.forhistiur.de/legacy/zitat/1109bond.htm. Accessed March 12, 2016.

Borofsky, Robert. 1997. Cook, Lono, Obeyesekere, and Sahlins. *Current Anthropology* 38(2): 255–265.

Bort, Julie. 2014. An Airbnb Host Got Drunk And Let Himself Into The House While A Business Insider Employee Was Sleeping. In *Business Insider*. http://www.businessinsider.com/bi-employee-has-airbnb-horror-story-2014-6. Published June 24, 2014. Accessed March 23, 2016.

Campbell, Ian. 1981. Of Polynesian Hospitality. *Journal De La Société Des Océanistes* 37(70–71): 27–37.

Chambers, Erve. 2000. *Native Tours: The Anthropology of Travel and Tourism.* Prospect Heights, Ill: Waveland Press.

Chesky, Brian. 2013 Untitled. http://blog.airbnb.com/test/. Published on September 12, 2013. Accessed November 16, 2015.

Das Statistik-Portal. 2016. Anzahl der Inserate von Airbnb-Unterkünften in Deutschland im Jahr 2015 nach Städte. http://de.statista.com/statistik/daten/studie/506272/umfrage/anzahl-der-inserate-von-airbnb-unterkuenften-in-deutschland-nach-staedte/. Accessed April 12, 2016.

Eberstadt, Nicholas. 1994. Demographic Shocks After Communism: Eastern Germany, 1989–1993. *Population and Development Review* 20(1): 137–152.

Florentin, Daniel. 2010. The 'Perforated City:' Leipzig's Model of Urban Shrinkage Management. *Berkeley Planning Journal* 23(1): 83–101. Accessed April 13, 2016. http://escholarship.org/uc/item/97p1p1jx.

Fulton, Wil. 2015. 11 Nightmarish Airbnb Horror Stories. https://www.thrillist.com/culture/airbnb-horror-stories-the-worst-airbnb-experiences-ever. Published on March 20, 2015. Accessed March 23, 2016.

Garcia-Zamon, Jean-Claude. 2008. *The Leipzig Model: Myth or Reality? A Study of City Management in the Former East Germany.* Lanham: University Press of America.

Hallowell, Roger, David Bowen, and Carin-Isabel Knoop. 2002. *Four Seasons Goes to Paris: "53 Properties, 24 Countries, 1 Philosophy".* Cambridge: Harvard Business School (business case).

Heyman, Josiah, and Howard Campbell. 2009. The anthropology of global flows: A critical reading of Appadurai's 'Disjuncture and Difference in the Global Cultural Economy'. *Anthropological Theory* 9(2): 131–148.

Hill, Steven. 2015 The Unsavory Side of Airbnb: How the popular matching company facilitates landlord conversion of entire rental buildings to de facto hotels. In *The American Prospect*. http://prospect.org/article/evictions-and-conversions-dark-side-airbnb. Published on October 19, 2015. Accessed May 5, 2016.

Ho, Erica. 2015. Why You Really Can't Trust Airbnb Reviews at All. In *Map Happy*. http://maphappy.org/2015/05/why-you-really-cant-trust-airbnb-reviews-at-all/. Published on May 14, 2015. Accessed January 16, 2016.

Hocart, A.M. 1952. The Divinity of the Guest. In *The Life-Giving Myth and Other Essays*, ed. Lord Raglan, 78–86. London: Methuen & Co.

Jhering, Rudolf von. 1887. Die Gastfreundschaft im Alterthum. In *Deutschen Rundschau* Vol. 9: 357–397. Accessed March 13, 2016. http://babel.hathi trust.org/cgi/pt?id=mdp.35112105488474.

Joyce, Morgan. 2016. STORYTIME: Airnbn HORROR stories. https://www.youtube.com/watch?v=ijH2h1SO2U4. Published on January 25, 2016. Accessed March 23, 2016.

Kämpfen, Victor. 1975. *Die Entwicklungsstadien der Entlöhnung der Bedienungsangestellten im Gastgewerbe, rechtlich und wirtschaftlich*. Bern: Herbert Lang and Peter Lang: Frankfurt am Main.

Kane, Herb Kawainui. 1997. Comment on "Cook, Lono, Obeyesekere, and Sahlins" by Robert Borofsky. *Current Anthropology* 38(2): 265–267.

Kim, Soo. 2016. Berlin Bans Thousands of Airbnb Properties. In *The Telegraph*. http://www.telegraph.co.uk/travel/destinations/europe/germany/berlin/articles/airbnb-listings-plummet-in-berlin-as-ban-comes-into-force/. Published May 3, 2016. Accessed May 5, 2016.

Kolinsky, Eva. 1998. In Search of a Future: Leipzig Since the Wende. *German Politics & Society* 16(4): 103–121.

Kotowski, Timo. 2014a. Wie deutsche Städte gegen Airbnb aufrüsten: Immer mehr Städte machen Front gegen das Internetportal Airbnb, das Zimmer auf der ganzen Welt vermittelt. Jetzt auch Frankfurt – die Stadt geht gegen die ersten Vermieter vor. In *Frankfurter Allgemeine Zeitung*. http://www.faz.net/aktuell/wirtschaft/netzwirtschaft/deutsche-staedte-kaempfen-gegen-die-vermittlungsboerse-airbnb-13239634.html. Published on October 31, 2014. Accessed April 16, 2016.

Kotowski, Timo. 2014b. In Berlin vermittelt Airbnb vor allem in Friedrichshain: Das Wohnraumvermittlungsportal Airbnb hat erstmals Zahlen zu seinem Deutschland-Geschäft vorgelegt. Es will den Vorwurf entkräften, für höhere Mieten mitverantwortlich zu sein. In *Frankfurter Allgemeine Zeitung*. http://www.faz.net/aktuell/wirtschaft/unternehmen/vermittlungsportal-airbnb-ver oeffentlicht-zahlen-fuer-berlin-13314208.html. Published on December 10, 2014. Accessed April 16, 2016.

Kusisto, Laura. 2015. Rent Your Place on Airbnb? The Landlord Wants a Cut. In *The Wall Street Journal*. http://www.wsj.com/articles/big-landlords-airbnb-discuss-partnerships-1450200473. published on Dec. 16, 2015. Accessed April 10, 2016.

Lieber, Ron. 2015. Airbnb Horror Story Points to Need for Precautions. In *New York Times*. http://www.nytimes.com/2015/08/15/your-money/airbnb-horror-story-points-to-need-for-precautions.html?_r=0. Published in August 14, 2015. Accessed March 23, 2016.

Lindholm, Charles. 1982. *Generosity and Jealousy: Swat Pukhtun of Northern Pakistan*. New York: Columbia University Press.

MacMillan, Douglas. 2013. Airbnb Starts Teaching Hospitality. In *The Wall Street Journal*. http://blogs.wsj.com/digits/2013/11/12/airbnb-starts-teaching-hospitality/. Published on November 12, 2013. Accessed May 5, 2016.

MetroFocus. 2016. Airbnb in NYC. http://www.thirteen.org/metrofocus/2016/01/airbnb-in-nyc/. Accessed February 2, 2016.

McNulty, Tracy. 2007. *The Hostess: Hospitality, Femininity, and the Expropriation of Identity*. Minneapolis: University of Minnesota Press.

Nuñez, Theron. 1989. Touristic Studies in Anthropological Perspective. In *Hosts and Guests: The Anthropology of Tourism*, ed. Valene L. Smith, 265–274. Philadelphia: University of Pennsylvania Press.

Neumann, Alexander, Manfred Zeiner, and Bernhard Harrer. n.d. *Wirtschaftsfaktor Tourismus in Stadt und Region Leipzig 2013*. Leipzig: Leipzig Tourismus und Marketing GmbH. Accessed April 15, 2016. http://www.leipzig.de/fileadmin/mediendatenbank/leipzig-de/Stadt/02.7_Dez7_Wirtschaft_und_Arbeit/80_Amt_fuer_Wirtschaftsfoerderung/1_Unternehmensservice/Broschuere_Wirtschaftfaktor-2013__final.pdf?L=0.

Parachutewoman. 2015. Comment on Reddit on an article by Zervas et al. 2015. https://www.reddit.com/r/AirBnB/comments/3kx1ko/a_first_look_at_online_reputation_on_airbnb_where/? Accessed March 23, 2016.

Pechlaner, Harald, and Frieda Raich. 2007. Wettbewerbsfähigkeit durch das Zusammenspiel von Gastlichkeit und Gastfreundschaft. In *Gastfreundschaft und Gastlichkeit im Tourismus: Kundenzufriedenheit und –bindung mit Hospitality Management*, eds. Harald Pechlaner and Frieda Raich, 11–24. Berlin: Erich Schmidt Verlag.

Pritchard, Annette, and Nigel Morgan. 2006. Hotel Babylon? Exploring hotels as liminal sites of transition and transgression. *Tourism Management* 27(5): 762–772.

Protalinksi, Emil. 2014. Airbnb Revamps its Review System: Hosts and Guests See Feedback Simultaneously, review period cut to 14 days. In *TNW*. http://thenextweb.com/insider/2014/07/10/airbnb-revamps-review-system-hosts-guests-see-feedback-simultaneously-review-period-cut-14-days/#gref. Accessed January 16, 2016.

Punter, David. 2012. *A New Companion to the Gothic*. Malden: Wiley-Blackwell.

Raglan, Lord, ed. 1952. Introduction. In *The Life-Giving Myth and Other Essays*, 6–8. London: Methuen & Co.

Rugh, Andrea B. 2009. *Simple Gestures: A Cultural Journey into the Middle East*. Washington, DC: Potomac Books.

Seebold, Elmar, ed. 2002. Kluge: Etymologisches Wörterbuch der deutschen Sprache. 24th ed. Berlin: Walter de Gruyter.

Sherlock, Kirsty. 2001. Revisiting the concept of hosts and guests. *Tourist Studies* 1(3): 271–295.

Shryock, Andrew. 1997. *Nationalism and the Genealogical Imagination: Oral History and Textual Authority in Tribal Jordan*. Berkeley: University of California Press.

Shryock, Andrew. 2004. The New Jordanian Hospitality: House, Host, and Guest in the Culture of Public Display. *Comparative Studies in Society and History* 46(1): 35–62.

Shryock, Andrew. 2012. Breaking Hospitality Apart: Bad Hosts, Bad Guests, and the Problem of Sovereignty. *Journal of the Royal Anthropological Institute* N.S.: S20–S33.

Sonia. 2014. Airbnb Nightmare: My Vacation was Held for Ransom. In *The Sonar Ping*. http://www.thesonarping.com/2014/02/airbnb-nightmare-my-vaca tion-was-held.html#.VvLht8eRbwy. Published on February 18, 2014. Accessed March 23, 2016.

Stadt Leizpig, Amt für Statistik und Wahlen. 1996. 3 01 Natürliche Bevölkerungsbewegung 1986 bis 1995. In *Statistisches Jarhbuch*. p. 37.

Stadt Leizpig. 2016a. "Einwohner" in Leipzig-Informationssystem LIS. http://statis tik.leipzig.de/statcity/table_print.aspx?cat=2&rub=1&tim= 31,30,29,28,27,26,25,24,23,22,21,20,19,18,17&per=y. Accessed April 12, 2016.

Stadt Leizpig. 2016b. "Geborene und Gestorbene" in Leipzig-Informationssystem LIS. http://statistik.leipzig.de/statcity/table_print.aspx?cat=3&rub=1&tim= 31,30,29,28,27,26,25,24,23,22,21,20,19,18&per=y. Accessed April 12, 2016.

Stadt Leizpig. 2016c. "Arbeitslose" in Leipzig-Informationssystem LIS. http:// statistik.leipzig.de/statcity/table_print.aspx?cat=7&rub=3&tim= 32,31,30,29,28,27,26,25,24,23,22,21,20&per=y. Accessed April 12, 2016.

Stone, Zak. 2015. Living and Dying on Airbnb: My dad died in an Airbnb rental, and he's not the only one. What can the company do to improve safety? In *Matter*. https://medium.com/matter/living-and-dying-on-airbnb-6bff8d600c04#.2ry0cn5xj. Published on November 8, 2015. Accessed February 20, 2016.

Sullivan, Danny. 2011. How Google Instant's Autocomplete Suggestions Work. http://searchengineland.com/how-google-instant-autocomplete-sugges tions-work-62592. Published on April 6, 2011. Accessed January 18, 2016.

Sundararajan, Arun. 2014. Peer-to-Peer Businesses and the Sharing (Collaborative) Economy: Overview, Economic Effects and Regulatory Issues. http://smallbusi ness.house.gov/uploadedfiles/1-15-2014_revised_sundararajan_testimony.pdf. Accessed November 16, 2015.

Taylor, Daron, and Jayne Orenstein. 2016. Why getting rid of tipping is better for everyone. In *The Washington Post*. https://www.washingtonpost.com/video/ business/why-getting-rid-of-tipping-is-better-for-everyone/2016/03/17/ 8a52cc60-ec45-11e5-a9ce-681055c7a05f_video.html. Published on March 17, 2016. Accessed May 5, 2016.

Wallner, Ernst Maxim. 1968. *Von der Herberge zum Grandhotel; Wirtshäuser und Gastlichkeit: Geschichte, Wirtshausnamen, Wirtshausschilder.* Konstanz: Rosgarten Verlag.

Warf, Barney, ed. 2010. Space of Flows. In *Encyclopedia of Geography*, Vol. 5, 2600–2601. Thousand Oaks, CA: SAGE Publications. Accessed April 2, 2016. http://remote.baruch.cuny.edu/login?url=http://go.galegroup.com. remote.baruch.cuny.edu/ps/i.do?id=GALE%7CCX1788301040&v=2.1&u= cuny_baruch&it=r&p=GVRL&sw=w&asid= aed2662304bfa321cc9082750cfdaa1f.

Wordweed. 2016. A Staycay Turned Sour: Our Airbnb Horror Story. http://wordweed.blogspot.com/2016/01/a-staycay-turned-sour-our-airbnb-horror.html. Published January 2, 2016. Accessed March 23, 2016.

Yannopoulou, Natalia, Mona Moufahim, and Xuemei Bian. 2013. User-Generated Brands and Social Media: Couchsurfing and AirBnb [sic]. *Contemporary Management Research* 9(1): 85–90.

Zanca, Russell. 2003. "Take! Take! Take!" Host-Guest Relations and All that Food: Uzbek Hospitality Past and Present. *The Anthropology of East Europe Review* 12(1): 8–16.

Zervas, Georgios, Davide Proserpio, and John Byers 2015 A First Look at Online Reputation on Airbnb, Where Every Stay is Above Average. http://poseidon01. ssrn.com/delivery.php?ID=105078117027007084031080088088 0 870640300640490340700490970921021120651100650941260950500000 060420100510530241030220270770240890190800350200330991151050 950751250300730560620460250280950890651250930980190131061150 950750050120871051250940970310051080220092&EXT=pdf. Published on April 12, 2015. Accessed March 23, 2016.

INDEX

© The Author(s) 2017   79
A. Touval, *An Anthropological Study of Hospitality*,
DOI 10.1007/978-3-319-42049-3

Printed in the United States
By Bookmasters